From Northamptonshire to Walker Valley

A History and Genealogy of the Weed Family

James H. Wiseman &
John L. "Jack" Weed

HERITAGE BOOKS
2019

HERITAGE BOOKS

AN IMPRINT OF HERITAGE BOOKS, INC.

Books, CDs, and more—Worldwide

For our listing of thousands of titles see our website
at
www.HeritageBooks.com

Published 2019 by
HERITAGE BOOKS, INC.
Publishing Division
5810 Ruatan Street
Berwyn Heights, Md. 20740

International Standard Book Number
Paperbound: 978-0-7884-3449-5

Dedication

I thank God for giving me the drive and determination to do this work. God's gifts are truly great. To dedicate this book to one person would be impossible so I would like to dedicate this to my parents, Reuben and Julia Dalpe Weed. My brothers, Daryl, Kyle and Scott and my cousin, Jim Wiseman. Last but not least, to my wife Jill and my step children, John and Kelsey Kober who have watched and toiled with me on my journey and without their love and support, this book would not have been possible.

I Love you all, Jack

Table of Contents

List of Illustrations

Foreword

To Jack Weed and all our family wherever they may be,

I hope you enjoy the information which Jack has amassed so carefully over the last couple of years. I know that he has poured a lot of time, effort and heart in this work. Without his dedication and caring, this tree could not have been compiled. If I have contributed in any small way in researching this work, it was my great pleasure.

Jim Wiseman

Mesa, AZ May 2006

Foreword II

In January 2002, my wife Jill and I walked down the famed Huguenot Street in New Paltz, NY. As we were walking and looking at the old stone houses, I began to think about my genealogy. I wondered if my family had ever lived here in these houses. Where did we come from? My great grandfather "Cap" Weed had always said that we were part Indian. I really didn't know the answers to these questions. I knew the line from myself to my great, great, great, great grandfather because my cousin, Jim Wiseman had told me the line. But who were these people and what did they do? After our little walk, we went home and I went to my computer and typed in the word "genealogy" in the search engine and my journey had begun.

What I had started was a four and a half year journey of spending countless hours looking at microfilm, going to cemeteries, road tripping to other counties and states. Meeting distant cousins in person, on the phone and online. I was also reacquainting myself with my own family. My aunts, uncles and cousins. Hearing stories that I have never heard and seeing life through their eyes. Also talking to older relatives and hearing stories about people that had been long gone.

My cousin Larry found out what I was doing and he gave me some advice, "There are things out there that are buried and should stay that way". In one aspect he is right. These people are dead and cannot defend themselves but also, it is about family and sometimes things are done that shouldn't be and maybe the future generations can learn and not make the same mistakes our ancestors did. Also, when I was at a local genealogical society doing research, I would always end up talking to someone about my family. It seemed that every family had a story. Every family had a scandal. Every family had skeletons in their closet. The more I researched, the more I found that this was life. Every family had problems, scandals, criminals and saints.

I didn't want to write a tell all book about scandals. I wanted to write a book about my genealogy and family. A family that I love and proud to be a part of. I also wanted the genealogical part of this book recorded because of 4 years of researching, no one had written it down. If you go online, nothing has been recorded on this part of the family. Jim and I wanted to be sure that all this work would be out there for the world to see and that no one else had to go through what Jim and I went through. It was labor but it was a labor of love. The highs of finding information and the lows of not finding anything. I had a great time doing this.

Since we are in the age of identity theft and fraud, we decided to only print 9 generations. We did not want to release any information of people that are still alive. Preserving our family's right to privacy and their own personal information was our concern. We were thinking that if we were still around in another 20 to 30 years, we may consider releasing another generation or 2 in a revised edition of this book.

To all who are researching the Weed family, good luck and hopefully you'll find something inside. If you don't, keep searching, the experience is rewarding.

Jack Weed
Walker Valley, NY May 2006

Jonas Weed: the first Weed in the New World

According to all records published in print or online, the first Weed to arrive in the new world was Jonas Weed who arrived in 1630 with Winthrop's fleet aboard the "Arabella" from England. He settled in Wethersfield, CT and in 1637, married a woman by the name of Mary. Mary's last name has been a subject of debate for years with no known proof. According to all records her last name was either Hoyt, Scofield or St. John. In 1641, Jonas and his family moved and became one of the first settlers of Stamford, CT. At the public records office in Northampton, citing records from the parish church for Chelveston in Northamptonshire, Jonas Weed was baptized February 20, 1597. Jonas died June 5, 1676 and his wife Mary died March 10 1689 in Stamford.

First Generation

1. **Jonas WEED** was baptized 20 Feb 1597 in Northhamptonshire, England. He died 5 Jun 1676 in Stamford, CT.

   Jonas married **Mary UNKNOWN**. Mary died 10 Mar 1689 in Stamford, CT.

   They had the following children:

	2	F	i.	**Elizabeth WEED** was born[1] about 1633 in Wethersfield, CT.
	3	F	ii.	**Mary WEED** was born[1] about 1639 in Wethersfield, CT.
	4	F	iii.	**Dorcas WEED** was born[1] about 1640 in Wethersfield, CT.
+	5	M	iv.	**John WEED** was born about 1643.
	6	M	v.	**Samuel WEED** was born[1] about 1645 in Stamford, CT.
	7	M	vi.	**Jonas WEED** was born[1] about 1647 in Stamford, CT.
	8	F	vii.	**Hannah WEED** was born[1] about 1650 in Stamford, CT.
	9	M	viii.	**Daniel WEED** was born[1] about 1652 in Stamford, CT.
	10	F	ix.	**Sarah WEED** was born[1] about 1654 in Stamford, CT.

---

[1] Connecticut Historical Society, Hartford, CT, Notes of Donald Lines Jacobus.

Second Generation

5. **John WEED** (Jonas) was born[1] about 1643 in Stamford, CT.

John married[1] **Joanna WESCOTT**.

They had the following children:

11	M	i.	**Jonas WEED** was born[1] 5 Feb 1667/1668 in Stamford, CT.
12	M	ii.	**Daniel WEED** was born[1] 11 Feb 1669/1670 in Stamford, CT.
+ 13	M	iii.	**John WEED** was born about 1675 and died 2 May 1739.
14	M	iv.	**Samuel WEED** was born[1] about 1677 in Stamford, CT.

---

[1]Connecticut Historical Society, Hartford, CT, Notes of Donald Lines Jacobus.

Third Generation

13. **John WEED** (John, Jonas) was born[1] about 1675 in Stamford, CT. He died[2] 2 May 1739 in Derby, CT.

John married[2] **Mary Jackson BEAMON** on 17 Dec 1702 in Derby, CT. Mary died[2] 27 Oct 1743 in Derby, CT.

They had the following children:

+   15   M   i.   **Samuel WEED** was born 18 Jul 1704.

       16   M   ii.   **John WEED** was born[1] 29 Sep 1706 in Derby, CT.

                         John married[1] **Alice CLARK** on 11 Sep 1735.

+   17   M   iii.   **Joseph WEED** was born 2 Nov 1708 and died 30 Nov 1771.

       18   M   iv.   **Jonas WEED** was born[1] 6 Apr 1711 in Derby, CT.

                         Jonas married[1] **Elizabeth STEVENS** on 15 Sep 1734.

       19   M   v.   **Caleb WEED** was born[1] 27 Dec 1714 in Derby, CT.

                         Caleb married[1] **Martha PECK** on 7 Jul 1742.

       20   M   vi.   **George WEED** was born[1] 20 Mar 1717 in Derby, CT.

                         George married[1] **Esther CLARK** on 23 Oct 1740.

       21   F   vii.   **Mary WEED** was born[1] 25 Mar 1719 in Derby, CT.

                         Mary married[1] **Unknown BEACH**.

       22   M   viii.   **Andrew WEED** was born[1] 27 Sep 1721 in Derby, CT. He died 12 Oct 1758.

---

[1] Connecticut Historical Society, Hartford, CT, Notes of Donald Lines Jacobus.
[2] Village of Derby, CT vital records.

23　F　　ix.　**Joanna WEED** was born[1] 22 Apr 1724 in Derby, CT.

Joanna married[1] **Amos OSBORN** on 15 Nov 1743.

Samuel Weed of Derby, CT: Counterfeiter

According to the public records of the state of Connecticut, Samuel Weed of Derby along with Daniel Tucker and Nathaniel Wooster in 1746 were arrested for counterfeiting. Weed and Tucker confessed to the charge while Wooster was found guilty by trial. Samuel Weed by pleading guilty to the charge, was sentenced to prison in Hartford, and had to forfeit all property real and personal. To add misery to this, his wife, Sarah Richardson died in 1748 while Samuel was still in prison. When Samuel was sentenced, Sarah returned to her childhood home of Waterbury, CT. Samuel was released in 1749 and was paroled with the knowledge that he could never leave Hartford County, CT ever again. If he left Hartford County and was caught, he was to be whipped 10 times and returned to prison. In 1750, Samuel violated his parole by leaving Hartford County and was caught. It was assumed that he left because his oldest son Samuel had died. There is no record if Samuel was whipped but it is obvious that he did not return to prison. In 1752, Samuel remarried and had 4 children. There is no record showing his death but by all records studied by this author, he had to die between 1760 and 1767.

Fourth Generation

15. **Samuel WEED** (John, John, Jonas) was born[1] 18 Jul 1704 in Derby, CT.

> BIOGRAPHY: In 1746, Samuel Weed along with Daniel Tucker and Nathaniel Wooster were arrested and indicted for counterfeiting. Weed and Tucker confessed to the charge while Wooster was found guilty by trial. Samuel Weed was sentenced to corporal punishment and forfeiture of all real and personal property to the government. In 1749, Samuel was released from prison and was never allowed to leave Hartford County, CT ever again. He was to report to the constable at any time. If he ever left Hartford County, he was to be whipped 10 times and returned to prison. In 1750, he left Hartford (presumably to attend his oldest son's funeral) and was caught and sent back to Hartford county. According to the public records, Samuel was never punished for leaving Hartford. The source of this information is The Connecticut Colonial Records from 1636-1776.

Samuel married[1] (1) **Sarah RICHARDSON** about 1730. Sarah was born[1] 28 Apr 1710 in Waterbury, New Haven, CT. She died[1] 15 Feb 1748 in Waterbury, New Haven, CT.

They had the following children:

    24   M   i.   **Samuel WEED** was born[2] 4 Mar 1731/1732 in Derby, CT. He died 1750 in Waterbury, CT.

    25   M   ii.   **David WEED** was born[2] 16 Jan 1733/1734 in Derby, CT.

+   26   M   iii. **Nathaniel WEED** was born 3 Jun 1736.

---

[1]Connecticut Historical Society, Hartford, CT, Notes of Donald Lines Jacobus.
[2]Village of Derby, CT vital records.

27 M iv. **Dan WEED** was born[2] 10 Nov 1738/1739 in Derby, CT. He died 1756 in Hartford, CT.

+ 28 M v. **Rueben WEED** was born 16 Oct 1740 and died 1792.

29 M vi. **John WEED** was born[2] 9 May 1742 in Derby, CT.

+ 30 M vii. **Abel WEED** was born 5 Nov 1744.

Samuel also married[3] (2) **Ruth UNKNOWN** in Hartford, Hartford, CT.

They had the following children:

31 F viii. **Sarah WEED** was baptized[3] 2 Sep 1753 in Hartford, CT.

32 F ix. **Jerusha WEED** was baptized[3] 30 Nov 1755 in Hartford, CT. She died[4] 20 May 1756 in East Hartford, CT.

+ 33 M x. **Samuel WEED** was born 13 Feb 1758 and died 31 Mar 1841.

34 M xi. **David WEED** was baptized[3] 10 Aug 1760 in Hartford, Hartford, CT. He died[5] 19 Jun 1825.

17. **Joseph WEED** (John, John, Jonas) was born[1] 2 Nov 1708 in Derby, New Haven, CT. He died[1] 30 Nov 1771.

Joseph married[1] **Deborah MOSES** on 5 Jun 1740 in Waterbury, New Haven, CT. Deborah was born 3 Nov 1718 in Simsbury, Hartford, CT. She died[1] 1810 in Granby, Hartford, CT.

They had the following children:

35 M i. **Isaac WEED** was born[1] 22 Mar 1741 in Simsbury, Hartford, CT.

36 M ii. **Aaron WEED** was born[1] 28 May 1742 in Waterbury, New Haven, CT.

37 M iii. **Moses WEED** was born[1] 5 Jan 1745 in Waterbury, New Haven, CT.

---

[3]Lucius Barnes Barbour, Families of Early Hartford, CT.
[4]Connecticut Historical Society, Hartford, CT, Records of the Center Church, Hartford, CT.
[5]Ancestry.com, New York Pensioners, 1835.

+   38   F   iv.   **Dorcas WEED** was born 19 Mar 1748.

     39   M   v.   **Joseph WEED** was born[1] 8 May 1757 in
                              Simsbury, Hartford, CT.

     40   M   vi.   **Benjamin WEED** was born[1] 18 Sep 1761 in
                              Simsbury, Hartford, CT.

The two Samuel Weeds of Newburgh, NY

There were 2 Samuel Weeds in Newburgh, NY at the same time. The one Samuel Weed was the son of Nathaniel Weed of Derby, CT who married Martha Kniffin. The other Samuel Weed was the son of Samuel Weed of Derby, CT (The counterfeiter) who married Abigail Gardner. The two Samuel Weeds' were related, Nephew and Uncle respectively. One of these Samuel Weeds' served in the Revolutionary war but as of this writing, there is no known proof which one served. The Sons of the American Revolution and the Daughters of the American Revolution are no longer accepting any applications for membership for Samuel Weed of Newburgh, NY until sufficient proof is found to see which one served. To complicate matters, each Samuel Weed had a son named Samuel but Samuel and Martha Kniffin Weed named their son Samuel Kniffin Weed and he used the name Samuel K. Weed the rest of his life to distinguish himself from the other Samuel Weeds'.

Fifth Generation

26. **Nathaniel WEED** (Samuel, John, John, Jonas) was born[1] 3 Jun 1736 in Derby, CT.

 He had the following children:

+   41   M   i.   **Samuel WEED** was born 1759.

28. **Rueben WEED** (Samuel, John, John, Jonas) was born[1] 16 Oct 1740 in Derby, New Haven, CT. He died[2] 1792 in Abbeville, Abbeville, SC.

 Rueben married[2] **Martha MESSOR** on 1759.

 They had the following children:

     42   M   i.   **Rueben WEED** was born[2] 1760 in Newburgh, Orange, NY.

     43   M   ii.   **Andrew WEED** was born[2] 11 Mar 1764 in Newburgh, Orange, NY.

     44   M   iii. **Nathaniel WEED** was born[2] 1768 in Newburgh, Orange, NY.

     45   F   iv.   **Martha WEED** was born[2] 1770 in Newburgh, Orange, NY.

30. **Abel WEED** (Samuel, John, John, Jonas) was born[1] 5 Nov 1744 in Derby, CT.

 BIOGRAPHY: From the book "Connecticut Divorces", authors Barbara Ferris and Louise Knox, copyright 1989, page 9, Weed, Dorcas of Simsbury, CT married 6 Feb 1766 to Abel Weed of Little Britain (Ulster County), NY until May 1767 - desertion and adultery with Ruth Weed, his father's wife. Petitioned 1 January 1773.

---

[1]Village of Derby, CT vital records.
[2]Louie Clarence Weed, Louie Gordon Weed, Southern Weeds and Allied Families, Gateway Press Inc, Baltimore, MD 1990.

Abel married[3] **Dorcas WEED**, daughter of Joseph WEED and Deborah MOSES, on 6 Feb 1767. The marriage ended in divorce. Dorcas was born[4] 19 Mar 1748 in Waterbury, New Haven, CT.

They had the following children:

    46 F   i. **Sarah WEED**.

33. **Samuel WEED**[5] (Samuel, John, John, Jonas) was born[6] 13 Feb 1758 in Hartford, Hartford, CT and was baptized[7] 19 Feb 1758 in Hartford, Hartford, CT. He died[6] 31 Mar 1841 in Newburgh, Orange, NY.

Samuel married[8] (1) **Abigail GARDNER** on 25 Jan 1781 in New Windsor, Orange, NY. Abigail was born[9] 22 Oct 1764 in Newburgh, Orange, NY. She died[9] 25 Apr 1810 in Newburgh, Orange, NY.

They had the following children:

+   47 F   i. **Elizabeth WEED** was born 25 Feb 1782.

+   48 M   ii. **Samuel WEED** was born 30 Dec 1783 and died 17 Feb 1863.

    49 F   iii. **Ruth WEED** was born[10] 22 Dec 1785. She died[10] 15 Dec 1795.

+   50 F   iv. **Sarah WEED** was born 16 May 1788 and died 25 Aug 1849.

    51 F   v. **Mary WEED** was born[10] 16 May 1788.

Mary married[11] (1) **Uriah STANTON**. Uriah

---

[3]Barbara Ferris, Louise Knox, Connecticut Divorces.
[4]Connecticut Historical Society, Hartford, CT, Notes of Donald Lines Jacobus.
[5]Genealogical Notes and Family records of Jonathan N.Weed.
[6]NSDAR. #320341 paper of Grace Weed Lippold
    #350470 paper of Grace Lippold Freeman
    #390905 paper of Alice Weed Johnson.
[7]Connecticut State Library, Hartford, CT, Records of the First Congregational Church, East Hartford, CT, Part 2 Page 902.
[8]New Windsor, NY Presbyterian Church Records.
[9]NSDAR, #350470 paper of Grace Lippold Freeman.
[10]NSDAR. #320341 paper of Grace Weed Lippold.
[11]NSDAR. #320341 paper of Grace Weed Lippold

died between 1810 - 1820.

Mary also married[11] (2) **Ebenezer STRICKLAND.**

+ 52 M vi. **Gardner WEED** was born 17 Feb 1790.

53 F vii. **Lydia WEED** was born[10] 8 May 1792.

Lydia married[11] **Silas C GARDNER.**

+ 54 M viii. **David WEED** was born 27 Jun 1794 and died 3 Oct 1827.

+ 55 F ix. **Anna WEED** was born 4 Aug 1796 and died 14 Aug 1859.

56 F x. **Christina WEED** was born[10] 17 Jan 1798. She died[10] 2 Sep 1802.

+ 57 F xi. **Jane WEED** was born 20 Sep 1801.

+ 58 M xii. **Silas Gardner WEED** was born 25 Apr 1804.

+ 59 F xiii. **Abigail WEED** was born 14 Aug 1806 and died 19 Apr 1855.

Samuel also married[6] (2) **Martha GARDNER** on 1 Nov 1810 in New Windsor, Orange, NY.

38. **Dorcas WEED** (Joseph, John, John, Jonas) was born[4] 19 Mar 1748 in Waterbury, New Haven, CT.

Dorcas married[3] **Abel WEED**, son of Samuel WEED and Sarah RICHARDSON, on 6 Feb 1767. The marriage ended in divorce. Abel was born[1] 5 Nov 1744 in Derby, CT.

> BIOGRAPHY: From the book "Connecticut Divorces", authors Barbara Ferris and Louise Knox, copyright 1989, page 9, Weed, Dorcas of Simsbury, CT married 6 Feb 1766 to Abel Weed of Little Britain (Ulster County), NY until May 1767 - desertion and adultery with Ruth Weed, his father's wife. Petitioned 1 January 1773.

They had the following children:

60 F i. Sarah WEED is printed as #46.

#350470 paper of Grace Lippold Freeman.

The Brick Wall is finally broken through!

For those of you who do not know what a brick wall is, it is the point of research that you cannot go any further. Jim and I knew that Samuel Weed (1783-1863) was our grandfather. This is as far as we could go because there was nothing written about this man. We found him in the 1850 census in the town of Mamakating in Sullivan County, NY. On a trip to the Sullivan county historical society in Hurleyville, NY, I noticed that in the 1855 NY census that Samuel Weed was born in Orange County, NY. According to the 1790 federal census, there were only 3 people that could have been his father. There were the 2 Samuel Weeds of Newburgh and Charles Weed in the town of Wallkill. After researching, I found that Charles Weed was married in 1796 so that counted him out. That left the 2 Samuel Weeds of Newburgh. I knew that one had married Martha Kniffin and the other had married Abigail Gardner. I also knew that 3 other people had tried to break down this brick wall and did not succeed.

According to 3 DAR applications, Samuel Weed (1783-1863) was the son of Samuel Weed and Abigail Gardner. These were only applications but upon reviewing them more, the source of their information was the family notes and records of Jonathan Noyes Weed (1825-1911). According to the applications, Samuel Weed (the father) was born about 1758/59/60 in Hartford, CT.

In the book, "Early families of Hartford, CT" by Lucius Barnes Barbour, there was a Samuel Weed in Hartford, CT who married a woman by the name of Ruth. As of this writing, her last name is unknown. Samuel and Ruth Weed had 4 children, Sarah born 1753, Jerusha born 1755, Samuel born 1758 and David born 1760.

All of this information led me to believe that the Samuel who married Ruth was the same Samuel Weed of Derby who was arrested for counterfeiting but there was no proof. I knew that Samuel was on parole and he could not leave Hartford for the rest of his life but in the Weed family, the name Samuel was incredibly common. There were a lot of Samuel Weeds' especially in Connecticut, so to pinpoint one of them seemed impossible.

The brick wall finally fell the day that Jim and I went to Hartford, CT to go to the Connecticut State historical society. As I was going through the notes of Donald Lines Jacobus, the famous Connecticut genealogical researcher, Jim had found the answer we were looking for.

It was found in the book "Connecticut Divorces" by Barbara Ferris and Louise Knox. On page 9 it was written that Dorcas Weed of Simsbury, CT who married Abel Weed of Little Britain (Now known as New Windsor), NY on 6 February 1766 until May 1767 filed for divorce because Abel had deserted her and was having sexual relations with Ruth Weed, his father's wife.

As Jim and I recovered from the shock, I realized that Abel Weed was the youngest son of Samuel Weed of Derby (the counterfeiter) and it was the same Samuel Weed who married the unknown Ruth in Barbour's book.

I believe it was only fitting that Jim broke down the wall. He had been researching the Weed family since 1968 after his grandfather's death. I was just happy to be there when the wall came tumbling down.

Sixth Generation

41. **Samuel WEED**[1] (Nathaniel, Samuel, John, John, Jonas) was born[1] 1759.

Samuel married[2] **Martha KNIFFIN**. Martha was born 1760.

They had the following children:

+   61   F   i.   **Mary WEED** was born 1776 and died 23 Aug 1850.

+   62   M   ii.   **Samuel Kniffin WEED** was born 11 Mar 1784 and died 14 Mar 1854.

47. **Elizabeth WEED** (Samuel, Samuel, John, John, Jonas) was born[3] 25 Feb 1782.

Elizabeth married[4] **John MARONEY**. John was born about 1784. He died[5] 30 Mar 1849 in New Windsor, Orange, NY.

They had the following children:

+   63   M   i.   **Samuel Weed MARONEY** was born 1800.

+   64   F   ii.   **Hester MARONEY** was born 13 Jan 1812 and died 24 Feb 1877.

+   65   M   iii.   **Uriah MARONEY** was born 1818.

      66   F   iv.   **Mahila MARONEY** was baptized[6] 30 Jun 1833 in Newburgh, Orange, NY.

---

[1]Genealogical Notes and Family records of Jonathan N.Weed.

[2]Frank L. Crawford, Morris D' Camp Crawford and his wife, Charlotte Holmes Crawford: their lives, ancestries and descendants, Frank L. Crawford, Ithaca, NY 1939, Page 38.

[3]NSDAR. #320341 paper of Grace Weed Lippold.

[4]NSDAR. #320341 paper of Grace Weed Lippold #350470 paper of Grace Lippold Freeman.

[5]Orange County, NY Genealogical Society, Vital records from the Newburgh Gazette.

[6]Gardnertown UMC, Newburgh, NY, Record of Baptisms, Orange County Genealogical Society, Goshen, NY.

48. **Samuel WEED** (Samuel, Samuel, John, John, Jonas) was born[7] 30 Dec 1783 in Orange County, NY. He died[8] 17 Feb 1863 in Walker Valley, Ulster, NY and was buried[8] in Walker Valley Cemetery, Walker Valley, NY.

> BIOGRAPHY: Samuel served in the War of 1812 from September to December 1814.

> OTHER: Samuel Weed had a granddaughter by the name of Christiann Weed. She was born 2 Aug 1832 and died 16 Oct 1853 in Burlingham, Sullivan, NY. She was buried in the Burlingham cemetery. Her parents as of this writing are unknown. According to her obituary in the "Whig Press" on Monday, October 24, 1853, she is listed as Samuel Weed's granddaughter.

Samuel married[9] **Olive BULLARD**, daughter of Nathan BULLARD and Rebecca FENTON, on 17 Jan 1805 in Pleasant Valley (Now Known as Plattekill), Ulster, NY. Olive was born[10] 3 May 1783 in Newburgh, Orange, NY. She died[10,11] 24 Feb 1879 in Walker Valley, Ulster, NY and was buried in Walker Valley Cemetery, Walker Valley, NY.

> Married by Rev. Levi Hall

Samuel and Olive had the following children:

+   67   M   i.   **Charles WEED** was born 7 Mar 1806 and died 28 Feb 1877.

+   68   M   ii.   **Samuel B WEED** was born 9 Dec 1809 and died 8 Jan 1890.

+   69   F   iii.   **Jane WEED** was born 3 Aug 1812 and died 13 May 1898.

+   70   F   iv.   **Harriet WEED** was born 10 Dec 1815 and died

---

[7] 1855 New York state census.
[8] Walker Valley, NY Cemetery.
[9] War of 1812 Pension File of Samuel Weed.
[10] Edgar J. Bullard, Bullard and Allied Families, American Historical Society, 1930.
[11] Ida Jane Weed Gibbs Family Bible.

20 Sep 1887.

+ 71 M v. **Nathan B WEED** was born 20 Dec 1818 and
died 30 Apr 1894.

72 M vi. **Henry WEED** was born 1820. He died[12] 14 Apr
1896 at the Ulster County Alms House, New
Paltz, Ulster, NY and was buried at the Ulster
County Alms House cemetery, New Paltz,
NY.

> At a ceremony on October 2,
> 2004, there was a dedication
> to the over 2500 people who
> died at the Ulster county
> Alms house. This dedication
> was spurred by the research
> of Susan Stessin-Cohn who
> started to research the
> Ulster county poorhouse in
> 2000. In essence, this was
> the funeral for all of those
> people who died and were
> buried there.

+ 73 M vii. **John WEED** was born 5 Jan 1822 and died 24
Dec 1893.

+ 74 M viii. **Levi WEED** was born 1 Feb 1824 and died 21
Apr 1907.

+ 75 M ix. **George William WEED** was born 22 Dec 1828
and died 19 Mar 1863.

50. **Sarah WEED** (Samuel, Samuel, John, John, Jonas) was born[3] 16
May 1788. She died[3] 25 Aug 1849 in Newburgh, NY and was
buried[13] in Gardnertown Cemetery, Newburgh, NY.

Sarah married[4] **John MILBURN**. John was born 1785. He died 28
Oct 1845 in Newburgh, NY and was buried[13] in Gardnertown
Cemetery, Newburgh, NY.

They had the following children:

+ 76 M i. **Samuel MILBURN** was born 24 Mar 1809 and
died 15 Feb 1849.

---

[12]New York state death certificate.
[13]Gardnertown Cemetery, Newburgh, NY.

+   77   M   ii.   **Isaac G MILBURN** was born 1812.

52.   **Gardner WEED** (Samuel, Samuel, John, John, Jonas) was born[3] 17 Feb 1790.

Gardner married[4] **Sarah REYNOLDS**. Sarah died[14] 1833.

They had the following children:

+   78   F   i.   **Lavinia WEED** was born 1815 and died 12 Jul 1897.

+   79   M   ii.   **Daniel R WEED** was born 1817 and died 22 May 1872.

54.   **David WEED** (Samuel, Samuel, John, John, Jonas) was born[3] 27 Jun 1794. He died[15] 3 Oct 1827 in Newburgh, Orange, NY.

David married[15] **Deborah NOYES** on 11 Jan 1816 in Newburgh, Orange, NY. Deborah was born[15] 13 Feb 1795. She died[15] 14 Dec 1867 in Newburgh, Orange, NY.

They had the following children:

    80   F   i.   **Celia WEED** was born[15] 1816.

           BIOGRAPHY: Celia never married.

    81   F   ii.   **Rebecca Noyes WEED** was born[15] 1817. She died[15] 13 Mar 1896.

           BIOGRAPHY: Rebecca never married.

---

[14] Genealogy.com, Orange Co., NY Message board # 1041.
[15] Orange County, NY Genealogical Society, Notes of Gertrude Watkins Gray.

Rebecca Noyes Weed

+ 82 M iii. **Daniel Tompkins WEED** was born 13 Mar 1820 and died 18 Aug 1901.

 83 M iv. **Thomas Noyes WEED** was born[15] 10 Jan 1822 in Newburgh, Orange, NY. He died[15] 13 Jan 1892 in St. Andrews, Orange, NY.

 Thomas married[5] **Mary E MERWIN**.

+ 84 F v. **Abigail WEED** was born 4 Dec 1823 and died 13 Mar 1879.

+ 86 M vii. **Jonathan Noyes WEED** was born 20 Nov 1825 and died 23 Feb 1911.

55. **Anna WEED** (Samuel, Samuel, John, John, Jonas) was born[3] 4 Aug 1796. She died[16] 14 Aug 1859 in Newburgh, NY and was buried[17] in St. Georges Cemetery, Newburgh, NY.

 Anna married[4] **Silas Bond GARDNER**. Silas was born[17] 27 Mar 1792. He died[17] 28 Aug 1875 in Newburgh, Orange, NY and was buried in St. Georges Cemetery, Newburgh, NY.

---

[16]Newburgh Daily News, Monday, August 15 1859.
[17]War of 1812 Pension File of Silas B. Gardner.

They had the following children:

    87 F   i.   **Mary GARDNER** was born about 1814. She died[5] 4 Mar 1853 in Newburgh, Orange, NY.

+   88 M   ii. **Levi Weed GARDNER** was born 1821.

+   89 F   iii. **Mahala GARDNER** was born 1822.

+   90 F   iv. **Martha Weed GARDNER** was born 7 May 1825 and died 12 Nov 1905.

    91 M   v.   **Andrew J GARDNER**[18] was born 1830 in New York.

57. **Jane WEED** (Samuel, Samuel, John, John, Jonas) was born[19,20] 20 Sep 1801.

Jane married **Hosea BROWN**[19,20]. Hosea was born[21] 1795 in New York.

They had the following children:

    92 M   i.   **Addison W BROWN** was born Sep 1817 in Newburgh, Orange, NY. He died[22] 28 Feb 1871 in Brooklyn, Kings, NY.

                   Addison married[23] **Ellen VANZILE** on 15 Aug 1839 in Newburgh, Orange, NY.

+   93 M   ii. **Nathaniel M BROWN** was born 30 Dec 1819.

+   94 M   iii. **Silas BROWN** was born Sep 1821.

+   95 F   iv. **Anna Eliza BROWN** was born 1830.

    96 M   v.   **Charles BROWN** was born[21] 1833.

+   97 F   vi. **Harriet BROWN** was born 1835.

    98 F   vii. **Matilda BROWN** was born[21] 1840.

---

[18]Will of Silas B. Gardner.
[19]NSDAR, #350470 paper of Grace Lippold Freeman.
[20]NSDAR, #390905 paper of Alice Weed Johnson.
[21]1860 Federal Census, Newburgh, Orange, NY.
[22]Brooklyn Daily Eagle, Tuesday, February 28, 1871, Page 7.
[23]Gardnertown UMC, Newburgh, NY Record of Marriages, Orange Co. Genealogical Society, Goshen, NY.

Matilda married[24] **Daniel GARDNER**.

58. **Silas Gardner WEED** (Samuel, Samuel, John, John, Jonas) was born[3] 25 Apr 1804.

Silas married[4] **Susannah LOCKWOOD**. Susannah was born 13 Oct 1803 in Newburgh, Orange, NY. She died[25] 13 Aug 1854 in Brooklyn, Kings, NY and was buried[25] in Green-Wood Cemetery, Brooklyn, NY.

They had the following children:

+   99   F   i.   **Martha Jane WEED** was born 12 Jan 1824 and died 7 May 1858.

+   100   M   ii.   **Robert Lockwood WEED** was born 1828.

+   101   F   iii.   **Frances M WEED** was born 1831.

    102   M   iv.   **Silas Lockwood WEED** was born[26] 1835.

    103   M   v.   **Samuel Lockwood WEED** was born 1839. He died[25,27] 19 Nov 1863 in Brooklyn, Kings, NY and was buried[25] in Green-Wood Cemetery, Brooklyn, NY.

    104   F   vi.   **Susan Ann WEED** was born 1841. She was buried[25] in Green-Wood Cemetery, Brooklyn, NY.

    105   M   vii.   **William T WEED** was born[26] 1844.

    106   F   viii.   **Caroline B WEED** was born[26] 1845.

59. **Abigail WEED** "Abbey" (Samuel, Samuel, John, John, Jonas) was born[3] 14 Aug 1806. She died[13] 19 Apr 1855 and was buried[13] in Gardnertown Cemetery, Newburgh, NY.

Abbey married[4] **Isaac LOCKWOOD**. Isaac was born[13] 15 Apr 1799 in Newburgh, Orange, NY. He died[13] 12 May 1870 and was buried[13] in Gardnertown Cemetery, Newburgh, NY.

---

[24]Portrait and Biographical record of Rockland and Orange Counties, NY, Chapman Publishing Co. 1895, Page 461.
[25]Records of Green-Wood cemetery, Brooklyn, NY.
[26]1850 Federal Census, Brooklyn, Kings, NY Ward 11.
[27]Brooklyn Daily Eagle, Thursday, November 19, 1863.

They had the following children:

107 M   i.   **Isaac Weed LOCKWOOD** was born[13,21] 30 Jan 1830. He died[13] 1 Apr 1851 and was buried[13] in Gardnertown Cemetery, Newburgh, NY.

108 M   ii.   **David S LOCKWOOD** was born[13] 27 Nov 1836. He died[13] 30 Jul 1838 and was buried[28] in Gardnertown Cemetery, Newburgh, NY.

109 M iii.   **William LOCKWOOD** was born[21] 1839.

110 M iv.   **Samuel W LOCKWOOD** was born[28] 7 Feb 1841. He died[28] 9 Aug 1848 and was buried[28] in Gardnertown Cemetery, Newburgh, NY.

111 F   v.   **Abby LOCKWOOD** was born[21] 1844.

112 F   vi.   **Mary LOCKWOOD** was born[21] 1846.

113 M vii.   **Charles LOCKWOOD** was born[21] 1848.

---

[28]Orange County, NY Genealogical Society, Records from Newburgh, New Windsor and other nearby towns.

Levi Weed: the first Weed in Walker Valley

According to the 1850 federal census, Levi Weed was living at the James Baker farm in Walker Valley as a laborer. His father, Samuel was living in Mamakating which is across the county line. On April 1, 1856, Samuel Weed purchased the James Baker farm where he lived until his death in 1863. Levi Weed would marry Mary Mance of Cragsmoor and live across the road from his parent's house.

Levi was a shoemaker by trade and had 4 children. Mary died at age 34 in 1866 leaving Levi to raise, Jeanette, James, George and Ida. Levi lived a long life and died at age 83 in 1907 at the Ulster county alms house in New Paltz, NY. He is buried alongside his wife in the Walker Valley cemetery.

In Walker Valley today, the red barn that was part of the Baker farm that was built by Levi Weed, still stands and the road by the barn is Red Barn Road. Levi Weeds' house was purchased by the Voshage family and when renovations were done to the house, old shoe soles were found underneath the flooring.

Seventh Generation

61. **Mary WEED** (Samuel, Nathaniel, Samuel, John, John, Jonas) was born[1] 1776. She died[2] 23 Aug 1850 and was buried[2] in Cedar Hill Cemetery, Newburgh, NY.

Mary married[1] (1) **Underhill MERRITT** on 6 Jun 1793. Underhill was born 1769. He died[1] 19 Nov 1804.

They had the following children:

+   114 F   i.   **Martha MERRITT** was born 8 Jul 1794 and died 14 Sep 1848.

+   115 M   ii.   **Josiah MERRITT** was born 21 Aug 1796 and died 23 Feb 1869.

+   116 M   iii. **Daniel MERRITT** was born 1799 and died 1867.

Mary also married (2) **Daniel BLOOMER**. Daniel died[2] 10 May 1808.

62. **Samuel Kniffin WEED** (Samuel, Nathaniel, Samuel, John, John, Jonas) was born[3] 11 Mar 1784. He died[3] 14 Mar 1854 in New Windsor, Orange, NY and was buried[4] in Little Britain Cemetery, New Windsor, NY.

Samuel married[3] **Sarah VAIL** on 20 Feb 1807 in New Hackensack, Dutchess, NY. Sarah was born[5] 10 May 1786. She died[5] 20 Jun 1860 and was buried[5] in Little Britain Cemetery, New Windsor, NY.

They had the following children:

117 M   i.   **Joseph WEED** was born[3] 20 Nov 1807. He died[3]

---

[1]Frank L. Crawford, Morris D' Camp Crawford and his wife, Charlotte Holmes Crawford: their lives, ancestries and descendants, Page 33.
[2]Frank L. Crawford, Morris D' Camp Crawford and his wife, Charlotte Holmes Crawford: their lives, ancestries and descendants, Page 34.
[3]William Penn Vail, M.D., Moses Vail Of Huntington, L.I., Unknown, 1947, Page 86.
[4]Genealogical Notes and Family records of Jonathan N.Weed.
[5]The Historical Society of Newburgh Bay and the Highlands, Genealogical Notes of Raphael A. Weed.

23 Nov 1824.

118   M   ii.   **Benjamin WEED** was born[3] 18 Jun 1809.

119   M   iii.   **Franklin WEED** was born[3] 18 Jun 1809.

120   F   iv.   **Elizabeth WEED** was born[3] 10 Apr 1811. She died[3] 15 Jul 1816.

+   121   M   v.   **Samuel WEED** was born 20 Feb 1813 and died 13 Nov 1898.

+   122   M   vi.   **Charles WEED** was born 23 Apr 1815 and died 23 Sep 1879.

123   F   vii.   **Sarah WEED** was born[3] 20 May 1817. She died[3] 24 Mar 1824.

+   124   M   viii.   **Nathaniel WEED** was born 27 May 1819 and died 11 Feb 1887.

125   F   ix.   **Mary WEED** was born[3] 3 Jan 1822. She died[3] 14 Aug 1825.

+   126   M   x.   **William Roe WEED** was born 26 Feb 1825 and died 8 Apr 1893.

127   F   xi.   **Caroline WEED** was born[3] 23 Aug 1828. She died[3] 30 Apr 1829.

63. **Samuel Weed MARONEY** (Elizabeth WEED, Samuel, Samuel, John, John, Jonas) was born[6] 1800 in New York.

Samuel married[6] **Mary UNKNOWN**.

They had the following children:

128   F   i.   **Abigail MARONEY** was born[6] 1828 in New York.

129   M   ii.   **Michael MARONEY** was born[6] 1828 in New York.

130   F   iii.   **Ann E MARONEY** was born[6] 1830 in New York.

131   F   iv.   **Mary MARONEY** was born[6] 1834 in New York.

132   F   v.   **Philinda MARONEY** was born[6] 1838 in New York.

---

[6]1850 Federal Census, Fishkill, Dutchess, NY.

133 M vi. **Uriah MARONEY** was born[6] 1837 in New York.

134 M vii. **W. Henry MARONEY** was born[6] 1838 in New York.

135 M viii. **Edward MARONEY** was born[6] 1844 in New York.

136 F ix. **Rachel MARONEY** was born[6] 1847 in New York.

64. **Hester MARONEY** (Elizabeth WEED, Samuel, Samuel, John, John, Jonas) was born[7] 13 Jan 1812. She died[8] 24 Feb 1877 and was buried[8] in Gardnertown Cemetery, Newburgh, NY.

Hester married **Samuel MILBURN**, son of John MILBURN and Sarah WEED. Samuel was born[7] 24 Mar 1809 in Newburgh, Orange, NY and was baptized[7] 30 Jun 1833 in Newburgh, Orange, NY. He died[8] 15 Feb 1849 and was buried[8] in Gardnertown Cemetery, Newburgh, NY.

They had the following children:

137 F i. **Sarah MILBURN** was born[9] 1829.

+ 138 F ii. **Abby Jane MILBURN** was born 4 Nov 1830 and died 23 Feb 1916.

+ 139 M iii. **Samuel J MILBURN** was born Apr 1835.

140 F iv. **Mariah G MILBURN** was born[9] 1838.

141 F v. **Catharine MILBURN** was born[9] 1839.

+ 142 F vi. **Martha MILBURN** was born 1843.

+ 143 F vii. **Margaret Ann MILBURN** was born 1847 and died 1911.

65. **Uriah MARONEY** (Elizabeth WEED, Samuel, Samuel, John, John, Jonas) was born[10] 1818 in New York.

Uriah married[10] **Emily UNKNOWN**.

---

[7]Gardnertown UMC, Newburgh, NY, Record of Baptisms.
[8]Newburgh Bay and Hudson Highlands, Records from Newburgh, New Windsor and other nearby towns, Vol 1.
[9]1860 Federal Census, Newburgh, Orange, NY.
[10]1850 Federal Census, Ramapo, Rockland, NY.

They had the following children:

144 F   i.   **Charlotte MARONEY** was born[10] 1841 in New York.

145 F   ii.   **Louisa MARONEY** was born[10] 1842 in New York.

+   146 M   iii. **George MARONEY** was born 1844.

147 M   iv. **Luther T MARONEY** was born[10] 1846 in New York.

> Luther also had an alias. He was known as Luther T. Conklin. He served in the 35th New Jersey Infantry in the Civil War.

148 M   v. **James MARONEY** was born[10] 1848 in New York.

149 F   vi. **Amanda MARONEY** was born[11] 1851 in New York.

150 M   vii. **Oscar W MARONEY** was born[11] 1855 in New York.

> Oscar married[12] **Carrie UNKNOWN**. Carrie was born[13,14] Sep 1859 in New York.

+   151 F   viii. **Sarah Elizabeth MARONEY** was born Apr 1856.

+   152 M   ix. **Nathan MARONEY** was born 1858.

67. Charles WEED (Samuel, Samuel, Samuel, John, John, Jonas) was born[15] 7 Mar 1806. He died[15] 28 Feb 1877 and was buried[15] in Bloomingburg Rural Cemetery, Bloomingburg, NY.

---

[11]1860 Federal Census, Ramapo, Rockland, NY.
[12]1880 Federal census, Nyack, Rockland, NY Dis 55.
[13]1880 Federal census, Nyack, Rockland, NY Dis 55.
[14]1900 Federal Census, Orangetown, Rockland, NY Dis 70.
[15]Bloomingburg Cemetery, Bloomingburg, NY.

Charles married[16] (1) **Elizabeth THOMAS**. Elizabeth was born[15] 31 Mar 1809. She died[15] 11 Jun 1873 and was buried[15] in Bloomingburg Rural Cemetery, Bloomingburg, NY.

They had the following children:

+   153   F   i.   **Sarah Ann WEED** was born 1830 and died 1 Sep 1889.

       154   M   ii.   **Henry Thomas WEED**[16] was born[17] 15 Mar 1832. He died[17] 27 Sep 1858 and was buried[17] in Walker Valley Cemetery, Walker Valley, NY.

                              Henry married[16] **Mary C BAKER.**

       155   M   iii.   **Odell WEED** was born 8 Dec 1834. He died[18] 18 Apr 1872 in Middletown, Orange, NY and was buried[19] in Hillside Cemetery, Middletown, NY.

+   156   M   iv.   **John Hollister WEED** was born 6 May 1837 and died 22 Aug 1921.

+   157   F   v.   **Mary E WEED** was born Sep 1840 and died 10 Jan 1908.

+   158   F   vi.   **Jane DuBois WEED** was born 13 Jan 1845 and died 26 Nov 1869.

       159   F   vii.   **Harriet Louisa WEED** was born[15] 7 Nov 1846 and was baptized[20] 29 Mar 1863 in Bloomingburg, Sullivan, NY. She died[15] 4 Apr 1870 and was buried[15] in Bloomingburg Rural Cemetery, Bloomingburg, NY.

                              BIOGRAPHY: Louisa never married

---

[16]Orange County, NY Genealogical Society, Notes of Elizabeth Horton.
[17]Walker Valley, NY Cemetery.
[18]Middletown Evening Press, Saturday, April 20 1872.
[19]Records of the Hillside cemetery, Middletown, NY.
[20]Methodist Episcopal Church of Bloomingburg, NY records of Baptisms.

Charles also married[21] (2) **Mary Evans HAMILTON** on 19 Oct 1874 in Bloomingburg, Sullivan, NY.

68. **Samuel B WEED** (Samuel, Samuel, Samuel, John, John, Jonas) was born[22] 9 Dec 1809. He died[23] 8 Jan 1890 in Matteawan, Dutchess, NY and was buried[24] in St. Luke's Cemetery, Beacon, NY.

Samuel married **Sarah Catherine EICHENBURGH**, daughter of James EICHENBURGH and Nancy SINSABAUGH. Sarah was born[22] 4 Oct 1819 in Montgomery, Orange, NY. She died[22] 27 Sep 1893 in Beacon, Dutchess, NY and was buried[22] in St. Luke's Cemetery, Beacon, NY.

They had the following children:

+   160   M   i.   **John Floyd WEED** was born 4 Sep 1839 and died 1 May 1909.

     161   M   ii.   **Almeren E WEED** was born 29 Jan 1844 in Phillipsport, Sullivan, NY. He died[25] 11 Feb 1847 and was buried[26] in Stanton Cemetery, Wurtsboro, NY.

+   162   M   iii.   **William Thair WEED** was born 1846 and died between 1875-1880.

+   163   M   iv.   **Ermon Romain WEED** was born 16 Nov 1848 and died 6 Jul 1921.

+   164   F   v.   **Mary R WEED** was born 7 May 1851 and died 26 Jun 1926.

     165   F   vi.   **Jeanette D WEED** "Nettie" was born[27] May 1855 in Phillipsport, Sullivan, NY. She died[28] 3 Nov 1924 in Poughkeepsie, Dutchess, NY and

---

[21]Orange County, NY Genealogical Society, Marriage Notices from the Goshen Independent Republican.
[22]St. Luke's Cemetery, Beacon, NY.
[23]New York state death certificate.
[24]Beacon Cemetery, Beacon, NY.
[25]Gertrude Barber, Sullivan County, NY Graveyard Inscriptions, Published 1930. Sullivan County Historical Society, Hurleyville, NY.
[26]Chester A Stanton Cemetery, Wurtsboro, NY.
[27]1900 Federal Census, Matteawan, Dutchess, NY Dist 10.
[28]City of Poughkeepsie, NY Vital records.

was buried[29] in Fairview Cemetery, Beacon, NY.

>   BIOGRAPHY: Jeanette never married.

+   166 F   vii. **Delaphine WEED** was born 3 Mar 1860 and died 18 Aug 1950.

69. **Jane WEED** (Samuel, Samuel, Samuel, John, John, Jonas) was born 3 Aug 1812. She died[30] 13 May 1898 in Ulsterville, Ulster, NY and was buried in Walker Valley Cemetery, Walker Valley, NY.

Jane married[31] **Isaac EVENS** on 7 May 1840. Isaac was born 1811 in Ulster Co., NY. He died[31] 26 Feb 1864 and was buried[17] in Walker Valley Cemetery, Walker Valley, NY.

>   Isaac served in the Civil War. He was with the 168th New York Volunteers, Company B.

>   Married by the Rev Stephen Strong at the residence of William J. Evens

Isaac and Jane had the following children:

167 F   i. **Elsie Ann EVENS** was born[32] 17 Feb 1841 in Evansville (Cragsmoor), Ulster, NY. She died[32] 12 Mar 1894 in New York, NY and was buried[17] in Walker Valley Cemetery, Walker Valley, NY.

>   Elsie married[17] **William DROMMOND**.

168 M   ii. **Andrew Jackson EVENS** was born 29 Mar 1844 in Cragsmoor, Ulster, NY. He died[33] 27 Aug 1922 in Middletown, Orange, NY and was buried[34] in New Prospect Cemetery, Pine Bush, NY.

---

[29]Fairview Cemetery, Beacon, NY.
[30]Town of Shawangunk, NY vital records.
[31]Civil War Pension files of Jane Weed Evens.
[32]New York, NY death certificate.
[33]Middletown Daily Times Press, Monday, August 28 1922.
[34]New Prospect Cemetery, Pine Bush, NY.

Andrew married[35] **Emily Upright EVANS**, daughter of Israel EVANS and Jane CRUVER, on 9 Mar 1898 in Walker Valley, NY. Emily was born[36] 1850 in Jamesburgh (now known As Walker Valley), Ulster, NY. She died 1902 and was buried[34] in New Prospect Cemetery, Pine Bush, NY.

+ 169 F iii. **Mary Josephine EVENS** was born 16 Sep 1848 and died 8 Aug 1930.

170 M iv. **George Nelson EVENS** was born[23,31] 20 Jan 1855. He died[23] 8 Feb 1933 in Goshen, Orange, NY and was buried[34] in New Prospect Cemetery, Pine Bush, NY.

171 M v. **Abner Franklyn EVENS** was born[31] 11 Sep 1857 in Cragsmoor, Ulster, NY. He died[37] 28 Apr 1924 in Middletown, Orange, NY and was buried[34] in New Prospect Cemetery, Pine Bush, NY.

BIOGRAPHY: Abner never married.

70. **Harriet WEED** (Samuel, Samuel, Samuel, John, John, Jonas) was born[38] 10 Dec 1815. She died[38] 20 Sep 1887 in Toledo, Lucas, OH and was buried[38] in Forest Cemetery, Toledo, OH.

Harriet married[39] **James H WOODEN**. James died May 1873 and was buried[40] 29 May 1873 in Forest Cemetery, Toledo, OH.

They had the following children:

172 F i. **Sarah A WOODEN**[41] was born 1841 in New York.

---

[35]Walker Valley, NY United Methodist Church records.
[36]1850 Federal Census, Shawangunk, Ulster, NY.
[37]Middletown Daily Herald, Tuesday, April 19 1924.
[38]Ohio State death certificate.
[39]Edgar J. Bullard, Bullard and Allied Families, American Historical Society, 1930.
[40]Records of the Forest cemetery, Toledo, OH.
[41]1850 Federal Census, Hillsdale, MI.

173 F ii. **Harriet J WOODEN**[41] was born 1845 in New York.

Harriet married[42] **Unknown BAER**.

174 M iii. **James H WOODEN JR**[41] was born 1848 in New York. He died[42] Sep 1909 in Toledo, OH and was buried[40] 20 Sep 1909 in Forest Cemetery, Toledo, OH.

175 F iv. **Ellen WOODEN**[41] was born 1849 in Michigan.

+ 176 F v. **Cynthia M WOODEN** was born Jul 1849.

177 M vi. **George B WOODEN**[43] was born 1852 in Michigan. He died[44] 7 Nov 1897 in Toledo, Lucas, OH and was buried[40] 30 Nov 1897 in Forest Cemetery, Toledo, OH.

George married[40] **Francis STEINMAN**.

178 F vii. **Emma E WOODEN**[43] was born 1855 in Michigan.

179 F viii. **Francis WOODEN**[43] was born 1858 in Michigan.

71. **Nathan B WEED** (Samuel, Samuel, Samuel, John, John, Jonas) was born[39] 20 Dec 1818 in Gardnertown, Orange, NY. He died[23] 30 Apr 1894 in Newburgh, Orange, NY and was buried[45] in Woodlawn Cemetery, New Windsor, NY.

Nathan married **Phebe TICE,** daughter of Philip TICE and Phebe HORTON. Phebe was born[39] 28 Jul 1814 in Phillipsport, Sullivan, NY. She died[46] 19 May 1894 in Newburgh, Orange, NY and was buried[45] in Woodlawn Cemetery, New Windsor, NY.

They had the following children:

180 F i. **Sarah C WEED** was born 28 Dec 1843. She died[47] 16 Jun 1898 in Newburgh, Orange, NY and was buried[45] in Woodlawn Cemetery,

---

[42]Toledo Daily Blade, Tuesday, September 21, 1909.
[43]1860 Federal Census, Hillsdale, MI.
[44]Toledo Daily Blade, November 8, 1897.
[45]The Newburgh News, Friday, July 29 1927.
[46]Newburgh Journal, Saturday, May 19 1894.
[47]Newburgh Daily Journal, Saturday, June 18 1898.

New Windsor, NY.

181 M ii. **Francis M WEED** was born 5 Apr 1845. He died[48] 28 Apr 1886 in Newburgh, Orange, NY and was buried[45] in Woodlawn Cemetery, New Windsor, NY.

182 M iii. **Jonathan N WEED** was born 10 May 1847. He died[49] 3 Jan 1905 in Newburgh, Orange, NY and was buried[45] in Woodlawn Cemetery, New Windsor, NY.

183 F iv. **Anna Eliza WEED** was born 28 Feb 1850. She died[45] 28 Jul 1927 in Newburgh, Orange, NY and was buried[50] in Woodlawn Cemetery, New Windsor, NY.

184 F v. **Emma Rette WEED** was born 12 Oct 1858. She died[51] 4 Feb 1936 in Newburgh, Orange, NY and was buried[50] in Woodlawn Cemetery, New Windsor, NY.

73. **John WEED** (Samuel, Samuel, Samuel, John, John, Jonas) was born[23] 5 Jan 1822 in Mamakating, Sullivan, NY. He died[23] 24 Dec 1893 in Cherry Creek, Chautauqua, NY and was buried[52] in Villenova Cemetery, Balcom, NY.

John married[53] **Elsie Anna PIERCE,** daughter of William PIERCE and Rachel ARNOLD, on 13 Nov 1856 in Villenova, Chautauqua, NY. Elsie was born Mar 1836. She died 1922 and was buried[52] in Villenova Cemetery, Balcom, NY.

They had the following children:

185 M i. **William George WEED** was born[54] 18 Mar

---

[48]Newburgh Journal, Thursday, April 29 1886.
[49]Newburgh Daily Journal, Wednesday, January 5 1905.
[50]Woodlawn Cemetery, New Windsor, NY.
[51]The Newburgh News, Tuesday, February 4 1936.
[52]Letter from Joyce Chase, Town Historian, Cherry Creek, NY.
[53]Whig Press Marriage Notices (1851-1865).
[54]Manuscript of David E Moon - Record of Moon, Pierce, Arnold and Holt families. Circa 1930. In possession of Patty Mallory, Houston, TX.

1857. He died[55] 20 Aug 1885 in Cherry Creek, Chautauqua, NY and was buried[52] in Villenova Cemetery, Balcom, NY.

186 F ii. **Ella Villetta WEED** "Ellie" was born[54] 18 Aug 1859. She died[55] 8 Jun 1881 in Cherry Creek, Chautauqua, NY and was buried[52] in Villenova Cemetery, Balcom, NY.

+ 187 F iii. **Annie Florilla WEED** was born 8 Dec 1860 and died 17 Feb 1905.

188 M iv. **Arthur Herbert WEED** was born[54] 21 May 1864 in Villenova, Chautauqua, NY. He died[54] 3 Oct 1947 in Jamestown, Chautauqua, NY and was buried[52] in Highland Cemetery, Cherry Creek, NY.

189 F v. **Harriet Jane WEED** "Hattie" was born[54] 22 Jun 1867 in Cherry Creek, Chautauqua, NY. She died 25 May 1955 in Skokie, Cook, IL.

Hattie married[54] (1) **Frederick GATES** on 13 Nov 1891. The marriage ended in divorce.

Hattie also married[52] (2) **William HUBER**.

190 F vi. **Minnie Gertrude WEED** "Gertie" was born[54] 18 Oct 1868 in Cherry Creek, Chautauqua, NY. She died[56] 7 Feb 1953 in Jamestown, Chautauqua, NY and was buried[56] in Villenova Cemetery, Balcom, NY.

Gertie married[52] **Unknown KEMP**. The marriage ended in divorce.

+ 191 F vii. **Myrtie Delia WEED** was born 18 Oct 1868 and died 14 Jan 1939.

192 F viii. **Elsie Rachel WEED** "Ettie" was born[54] 2 Aug 1871 in Cherry Creek, Chautauqua, NY. She died[55] 26 Sep 1879 in Villenova, Chautauqua, NY and was buried in Villenova Cemetery, Balcom, NY.

+ 193 M ix. **Herbert Odell WEED** was born 7 Jan 1874 and

---

[55]Villenova, NY cemetery records.
[56]USgenweb.org, Cemetery records of Villenova, NY cemetery.

died 3 May 1942.

74. **Levi WEED** (Samuel, Samuel, Samuel, John, John, Jonas) was born[57] 1 Feb 1824 in Mamakating, Sullivan, NY and was baptized[20] 25 Feb 1867 in Bloomingburg, Sullivan, NY. He died[23] 21 Apr 1907 in Ulster County Alms House, New Paltz, Ulster, NY and was buried[58] in Walker Valley Cemetery, Walker Valley, NY.

Levi married[57] **Mary MANCE**, daughter of Jacob MANCE and Aintje SCOTT, on 2 Dec 1851. Mary was born[57] 18 Jul 1831. She died[57] 2 Feb 1866 and was buried[17] in Walker Valley Cemetery, Walker Valley, NY.

They had the following children:

    194 F   i. **Rosena Jeanette WEED** was born[57] 3 Jun 1852 in Walker Valley, Ulster, NY and was baptized[20] 25 Feb 1867 in Bloomingburg, Sullivan, NY. She died[59] 20 Feb 1923 in Pine Bush, Orange, NY and was buried[34] in New Prospect Cemetery, Pine Bush, NY.

                    Rosena married[57] (1) **Namon DRAKE** on 1 Feb 1871 in Pine Bush, Orange, NY. The marriage ended in divorce.

                    Rosena also married[60] (2) **Myron THOMAS** on 20 May 1875 in Ithaca, Tompkins, NY. The marriage ended in divorce.

                    Rosena also married[61] (3) **George W ROCKWELL** on 28 Nov 1886 in Pine Bush, Orange, NY.

+   195 M   ii. **James Marshall WEED** was born 6 Jul 1857 and died 19 Feb 1926.

+   196 M   iii. **George E WEED** was born 15 Mar 1860 and died 13 Aug 1926.

+   197 F   iv. **Ida Jane WEED** was born 1 Nov 1862 and died

---

[57]Ida Jane Weed Gibbs Family Bible.
[58]Walker Valley, NY cemetery records.
[59]Middletown Daily Times Press, Saturday, February 24 1923.
[60]Civil War pension file of Myron Thomas.
[61]Middletown Daily Press, Tuesday, November 30 1886.

15 Sep 1934.

75. **George William WEED** (Samuel, Samuel, Samuel, John, John, Jonas) was born 22 Dec 1828 in Mamakating, Sullivan, NY. He died[62] 19 Mar 1863 in Newburgh, Orange, NY and was buried[17] in Walker Valley Cemetery, Walker Valley, NY.

George married[16] **Ann Eliza BROWN**. Ann was born 23 Feb 1840 in Newburgh, Orange, NY. She died[63] 2 Jun 1925 in Rensselaer, Rensselaer, NY and was buried in Albany Rural Cemetery, Albany, NY.

They had the following children:

    198 F   i. **Georgianna WEED** was born[64] Jun 1862. She died[65] 18 Sep 1939 in Poughkeepsie, Dutchess, NY and was buried[65] in Albany Rural Cemetery, Albany, NY.

    199 M   ii. **Oliver WEED** was born[66] 1863 in New York.

76. **Samuel MILBURN** (Sarah WEED, Samuel, Samuel, John, John, Jonas) was born[7] 24 Mar 1809 in Newburgh, Orange, NY and was baptized[7] 30 Jun 1833 in Newburgh, Orange, NY. He died[8] 15 Feb 1849 and was buried[8] in Gardnertown Cemetery, Newburgh, NY.

Samuel married **Hester MARONEY**, daughter of John MARONEY and Elizabeth WEED. Hester was born[7] 13 Jan 1812. She died[8] 24 Feb 1877 and was buried[8] in Gardnertown Cemetery, Newburgh, NY.

They had the following children:

    200 F   i. Sarah MILBURN is printed as #137.

+   201 F   ii. Abby Jane MILBURN is printed as #138.

+   202 M   iii. Samuel J MILBURN is printed as #139.

    203 F   iv. Mariah G MILBURN is printed as #140.

    204 F   v. Catharine MILBURN is printed as #141.

---

[62]Orange County, NY surrogate court.
[63]Email from Donna Radz, 1 Nov 2004.
[64]1900 Federal Census, Rensselaer, Rensselaer, NY Dis 53.
[65]Albany Rural cemetery, Albany, NY cemetery records.
[66]1870 Federal Census, Greenbush, Rensselaer, NY.

+ 205 F vi. Martha MILBURN is printed as #142.

+ 206 F vii. Margaret Ann MILBURN is printed as #143.

77. **Isaac G MILBURN** (Sarah WEED, Samuel, Samuel, John, John, Jonas) was born[7] 1812 in Newburgh, Orange, NY and was baptized[7] 30 Jun 1833 in Newburgh, Orange, NY.

Isaac married[67] **Sophia SHAY** on 16 Feb 1833 in Newburgh, Orange, NY.

They had the following children:

+ 207 M i. **Charles Wesley MILBURN** was born 1834.

     208 M ii. **Isaac I MILBURN** was born[9] 8 Aug 1838. He died[8] 28 Mar 1839 and was buried[8] in Gardnertown Cemetery, Newburgh, NY.

     209 M iii. **Willmot T MILBURN** was born 13 Mar 1844. He died[8] 31 Jan 1845 and was buried[8] in Gardnertown Cemetery, Newburgh, NY.

     210 F iv. **Sophia D MILBURN** was born[9] 1847.

     211 F v. **Louella MILBURN** was born[68] 1853.

78. **Lavinia WEED**[28] (Gardner, Samuel, Samuel, John, John, Jonas) was born 1815. She died[69] 12 Jul 1897 in Poughkeepsie, Dutchess, NY and was buried[69] in Poughkeepsie Rural Cemetery, Poughkeepsie, NY.

---

[67]Gardnertown UMC, Newburgh, NY Record of Marriages.
[68]1870 Federal Census, Warren, Rockland, NY.
[69]Records of Poughkeepsie Rural Cemetery, Poughkeepsie, NY.

Lavinia Weed Roberts

Lavinia married[70] **John ROBERTS** on 31 Dec 1832 in Bloomingburg, Sullivan, NY. John was born[69] 5 May 1808. He died[69] 27 Apr 1890 in Poughkeepsie, Dutchess, NY and was buried[69] in Poughkeepsie Rural Cemetery, Poughkeepsie, NY.

They had the following children:

+   212   F   i.   **Adaline ROBERTS** was born 1836 and died 12 Nov 1872.

+   213   M   ii.   **Benjamin ROBERTS** was born 1838.

+   214   F   iii.   **Sarah R ROBERTS** was born Apr 1841.

     215   M   iv.   **Henry ROBERTS** was born[71] 1843 in New York.

+   216   M   v.   **John J ROBERTS** was born 1846 and died 13 Apr 1912.

     217   M   vi.   **Charles ROBERTS** was born 1849. He died[69] 10 Jul 1910 in Poughkeepsie, Dutchess, NY and

---

[70]Records of the Reformed Protestant Dutch Church, Bloomingburg, NY, Record of Marriages.
[71]1850 Federal Census, Poughkeepsie, Dutchess, NY.

was buried[69] in Poughkeepsie Rural Cemetery, Poughkeepsie, NY.

+   218   F   vii.   **Phebe Ann ROBERTS** was born Sep 1850 and died between 1920-1930.

79. **Daniel R WEED** (Gardner, Samuel, Samuel, John, John, Jonas) was born 1817 in New York. He died[72] 22 May 1872 in Fishkill, Dutchess, NY and was buried[72] in Balmville Cemetery, Newburgh, NY.

Daniel married **Rebecca UNKNOWN**. Rebecca was born[73] 1824 in New York.

They had the following children:

     219   F   i.   **Emma WEED** was born[73] 1838 in New York.

     220   M   ii.   **Jacob C WEED** was born[73] 1841 in New York.

                   Jacob married[74] **Sarah UNKNOWN**.

     221   F   iii.   **Eliza WEED** was born[73] 1843 in New York.

     222   F   iv.   **Joanna WEED** was born[73] 1849 in New York.

     223   M   v.   **Sanford WEED** was born[75] 1854 in New York.

     224   F   vi.   **Theresa WEED** was born[75] 1855 in New York.

     225   F   vii.   **Louisa WEED** was born[75] 1857 in New York.

                   Louisa married[76] **Sylvester CONKLIN**. Sylvester was born[76] 1850 in New York.

+   226   M   viii.   **Daniel R WEED** was born 1858.

82. **Daniel Tompkins WEED** (David, Samuel, Samuel, John, John, Jonas) was born[77] 13 Mar 1820 in Bethlehem, Orange, NY. He died[77] 18 Aug 1901 in Newburgh, Orange, NY and was buried[78] in Cedar Hill Cemetery, Newburgh, NY.

---

[72]Newburgh Daily Journal, Friday, May 24, 1872.
[73]1850 Federal Census, Haverstraw, Rockland, NY.
[74]1860 Federal Census, Warren, Rockland, NY.
[75]1860 Federal Census, Fishkill, Dutchess, NY.
[76]1880 Federal census, Fishkill, Dutchess, NY Dis 38.
[77]Orange County, NY Genealogical Society, Notes of Gertrude Watkins Gray.
[78]Daniel Tompkins Weed Family Bible.

Daniel Tompkins Weed

Daniel married[78] **Elizabeth Ann WESTLAKE** on 16 Jun 1840. Elizabeth was born[79] 28 Oct 1821. She died[79] 26 Nov 1899 and was buried[78] in Cedar Hill Cemetery, Newburgh, NY.

```
Married by Rev. R. Wymond
```

Daniel and Elizabeth had the following children:

+   227   F   i.   **Juliette WEED** was born 24 Mar 1843 and died 20 Mar 1906.

+   228   M   ii.   **Jonathan Irving WEED** was born 26 Feb 1846 and died 4 Nov 1932.

     229   M   iii.   **Alonso WEED** was born[78] 26 May 1849. He died[78] 18 Dec 1850 and was buried[80] in Balmville Cemetery, Newburgh, NY.

     230   F   iv.   **Alice WEED** was born[78] 13 Jan 1851. She died[78]

---

[79]Daniel Tompkins Weed Family Bible.
[80]Orange County, NY Genealogical Society, Records from Newburgh, New Windsor and other nearby towns.

8 Apr 1851 and was buried[80] in Balmville Cemetery, Newburgh, NY.

+ 231 M v. **Adolphus WEED** was born 3 Apr 1852 and died 25 Jul 1934.

232 F vi. **Emma T WEED** was born[78] 3 Feb 1854. She died[78] 6 Jun 1940 and was buried[78] in Cedar Hill Cemetery, Newburgh, NY.

Emma married[79] **Joseph A SIMPSON** on 22 Jun 1887. Joseph died 11 Mar 1909 and was buried[79] in Woodlawn Cemetery, New Windsor, NY.

84. **Abigail WEED** (David, Samuel, Samuel, John, John, Jonas) was born[77] 4 Dec 1823 in Mamakating, Sullivan, NY. She died[77] 13 Mar 1879 in Walden, Orange, NY and was buried[77] in Wallkill Valley Cemetery, Walden, NY.

Abigail married[77] **Edward DUNN** on 8 Feb 1847 in Mamakating, Sullivan, NY. Edward was born 28 Dec 1825 in Plattekill, Ulster, NY. He died 16 Jan 1892 in Walden, Orange, NY and was buried[77] in Wallkill Valley Cemetery, Walden, NY.

They had the following children:

+ 233 F i. **Mary DUNN** was born 25 Mar 1850 and died 18 Jun 1896.

234 F ii. **Cornelia Independence DUNN** was born[77] 4 Jul 1852 in Middle Hope, Orange, NY. She died[77] 1922 and was buried[77] in Wallkill Valley Cemetery, Walden, NY.

+ 235 M iii. **Alphonso Weed DUNN** was born 14 Mar 1854 and died 30 Aug 1930.

+ 236 M iv. **David Lamorn DUNN** was born 7 Aug 1856 and died 1916.

237 M v. **Jonathan Noyes DUNN** was born[77] 16 Jul 1858 in Johnstown, Barry, MI. He died[77] 17 Oct 1911 in Walden, Orange, NY.

Jonathan married (1) **Priscilla TERWILLIGER**[77].

Jonathan also married (2) **Josephine Bodley MILLER**[77].

+   238   F   vi.   Emma Rebecca DUNN was born 1 Jul 1863.

86. **Jonathan Noyes WEED** (David, Samuel, Samuel, John, John, Jonas) was born[77] 20 Nov 1825. He died[77] 23 Feb 1911.

Jonathan Noyes Weed

Jonathan married[77] **Elizabeth Merritt GOODSELL** on 1851. Elizabeth was born[77] 18 Dec 1824. She died[77] 5 Jan 1890.

They had the following children:

    244   F   i.   **Ella WEED** was born[83,84] 27 Jan 1853 in
                       Newburgh, Orange, NY. She died[84] 10 Jan
                       1894.

    245   M   ii.   **Charles G WEED** was born[83,85] 31 Jul 1855.

    246   M   iii. **Frank WEED** was born[86] 1861.

88. **Levi Weed GARDNER**[87] (Anna WEED, Samuel, Samuel, John,

---

[83]1860 Federal Census, Newburgh, Orange, NY.
[84]The Historical Society of Newburgh Bay and the Highlands, Biography of Ella Weed.
[85]1900 Federal Census, Newburgh, NY 4th Ward.
[86]1870 Federal Census, Newburgh, Orange, NY, Ward 1.

John, Jonas) was born 1821.

Levi married **Martha UNKNOWN**. Martha was born 1825 in New York.

They had the following children:

247   F   i.   **Sarah M GARDNER** was born[88] 1842 in New York.

248   M   ii.   **Wesley G GARDNER** was born[88] 1844 in New York.

249   F   iii.   **Mary E GARDNER** was born[88] 1846 in New York.

250   M   iv.   **William G GARDNER** was born[88] 1847 in New York.

251   M   v.   **Richard L GARDNER** was born[88] 1849 in New York.

```
In the 1880 census, Richard
is listed with paralysis.
```

+   252   M   vi.   **Silas GARDNER** was born 1852.

+   253   F   vii.   **Alpharetta GARDNER** was born Jul 1854.

254   M   viii.   **Charles E GARDNER** was born[89] 1857 in New Jersey.

255   M   ix.   **Levi G GARDNER** was born[90] 1861 in New Jersey.

256   M   x.   **James H GARDNER** was born[90] 1863 in New Jersey.

257   F   xi.   **Anna I GARDNER** was born[90] 1865 in New Jersey.

258   M   xii.   **Frank GARDNER** was born[91] 1870 in New

---

[87]Will of Silas B. Gardner.
[88]1850 Federal Census, Perth Amboy, Middlesex, NJ.
[89]1860 Federal Census, Perth Amboy, Middlesex, NJ.
[90]1870 Federal Census, Perth Amboy, Middlesex, NJ.
[91]1880 Federal census, Perth Amboy, Middlesex, NJ

Jersey.

89. **Mahala GARDNER**[87] (Anna WEED, Samuel, Samuel, John, John, Jonas) was born[9] 1822 in New York.

Mahala married[67] **John W THOMAS** on 18 Dec 1843. John was born[9] 1824 in New York.

They had the following children:

+   259   M   i.   **Anthony S THOMAS** was born 1845.

     260   F   ii.   **Anna Maria THOMAS** was born[9] 1847 in New York.

90. **Martha Weed GARDNER**[87] (Anna WEED, Samuel, Samuel, John, John, Jonas) was born[92] 7 May 1825 in Newburgh, Orange, NY. She died[93,94] 12 Nov 1905 in Topeka, Shawnee, KS and was buried[93] in Topeka Cemetery, Topeka, KS.

Martha married[67] **James R WEAR** on 25 Feb 1846. James was born[93] 7 May 1824 in Orange County, NY. He died[93,95] 31 Dec 1894 in Eureka Springs, Carroll, AR and was buried[93] in Topeka Cemetery, Topeka, KS.

They had the following children:

     261   F   i.   **Martha J WEAR** was born[96] 1847 in New York.

     262   F   ii.   **Josephine WEAR** was born[96] 1848 in New York.

     263   M   iii.   **James R WEAR** was born[96] 1851 in New York. He died between 1920-1930.

No Children

James married[97] **Annie M BYERS** on 28 Jun 1881 in Topeka, Shawnee, KS.

+   264   F   iv.   **Abbey S WEAR** was born 16 Nov 1852 and died

---

Dis 129.
[92] 1900 Federal Census, Topeka, Shawnee, KS Ward 4 Dis 162.
[93] Records of the Topeka, KS cemetery.
[94] Topeka Daily Capital, Monday, November 13, 1905.
[95] Topeka Daily Capital, Wednesday, January 2, 1895.
[96] 1860 Federal Census, Pittston, Luzerne, PA.
[97] Shawnee county, KS Marriage records.

3 Oct 1881.

    265 M   v.   **Francis E WEAR** was born[93,96,98] May 1857 in Pittston, Luzerne, PA. He died[93] 6 Aug 1923 in Topeka, Shawnee, KS and was buried[93] in Topeka Cemetery, Topeka, KS.

                  Francis married **Mary F UNKNOWN**. Mary was born[98] Jun 1863 in Indiana.

    266 F   vi.   **Emeline WEAR** was born[96] 1859 in Pittston, Luzerne, PA.

    267 F   vii.   **Adelaide M WEAR.**

                  Adelaide married[97] **William T CLARK** on 30 Oct 1882 in Topeka, Shawnee, KS.

+   268 F   viii.   **Ina R WEAR** was born Aug 1862 and died between 1900-1904.

+   269 M   ix.   **Theodore Graham WEAR** was born 22 Aug 1865 and died 22 May 1931.

+   270 M   x.   **Norman S WEAR** was born Mar 1868 and died 21 Feb 1932.

93. **Nathaniel M BROWN** (Jane WEED, Samuel, Samuel, John, John, Jonas) was born[99] 30 Dec 1819 in Newburgh, Orange, NY.

Nathaniel married[67,99] **Caroline MERRITT** on 23 Feb 1842 in Newburgh, Orange, NY.

They had the following children:

    271 F   i.   **Adelia BROWN** [99] was born[9] 1844 in Newburgh, Orange, NY.

    272 M   ii.   **Albert BROWN** was born[9] 1847 in Newburgh, Orange, NY.

+   273 F   iii.   **Ellen V BROWN** was born 19 Feb 1850 and died 17 Dec 1909.

    274 F   iv.   **Adelaide BROWN** [99] was born[83] 1852 in Newburgh, Orange, NY.

---

[98]1900 Federal Census, Topeka, Shawnee, KS Ward 6 Dis 166.
[99]Portrait and Biographical record of Rockland and Orange Counties, Page 461.

275　F　　v.　**Jessie BROWN** was born[83] 1854 in Newburgh, Orange, NY.

276　M　　vi.　**Spencer G BROWN** was born[83,100] Dec 1857 in Newburgh, Orange, NY.

Spencer married[100] **Annie UNKNOWN**. Annie was born[100] Feb 1871 in New York.

277　F　　vii.　**Henrietta BROWN** [99] was born[101] 1859 in Newburgh, Orange, NY.

278　F　　viii.　**Anna BROWN** was born[83] May 1860 in Newburgh, Orange, NY.

279　F　　ix.　**Caroline BROWN** was born[101] 1863 in Newburgh, Orange, NY.

280　F　　x.　**Amy J BROWN** [99] was born[101,102] Feb 1869 in New Windsor, Orange, NY.

281　F　　xi.　**Tressa BROWN**[99].

94. **Silas BROWN** (Jane WEED, Samuel, Samuel, John, John, Jonas) was born[103] Sep 1821.

Silas married **Mary Ann VANGILE**.

They had the following children:

282　F　　i.　**Mary BROWN** was born[83] 1843 in Newburgh, Orange, NY.

283　F　　ii.　**Lavinia BROWN** was born[9] 1845 in Newburgh, Orange, NY.

284　M　　iii.　**Mervin BROWN** was born[9] 1849 in Newburgh, Orange, NY.

+　　285　M　　iv.　**Silas BROWN** was born 11 Apr 1854 and died 19 Jan 1927.

286　M　　v.　**Alfred BROWN** was born[83] 1857 in Newburgh, Orange, NY.

---

[100]1900 Federal Census, Newburgh, Orange, NY Ward 5 Dis 42.
[101]1870 Federal Census, New Windsor, Orange, NY.
[102]1900 Federal Census, New Windsor, Orange, NY Dis 47.
[103]1900 Federal Census, Wappingers Falls, Dutchess, NY Dis 44.

287 F vi. **Laura BROWN** was born[83] Apr 1860 in Newburgh, Orange, NY.

288 M vii. **Edward BROWN** was born[104] 1861 in New York.

289 F viii. **Delia BROWN** was born[104] 1870 in New York.

95. **Anna Eliza BROWN** (Jane WEED, Samuel, Samuel, John, John, Jonas) was born[9] 1830.

Anna married[99] **Isaac Garrison WHITE**.

They had the following children:

290 F i. **Ida WHITE** was born[83] 1857 in Newburgh, Orange, NY.

291 M ii. **James C WHITE** was born[83] 1859 in Newburgh, Orange, NY.

292 F iii. **Irena WHITE** was born[86] 1865 in Newburgh, Orange, NY.

97. **Harriet BROWN** (Jane WEED, Samuel, Samuel, John, John, Jonas) was born[9] 1835.

Harriet married[99] **John WHITE**.

They had the following children:

293 F i. **Georgie Anne WHITE** was born[105] 1864.

294 F ii. **Hattie WHITE** was born[105] 1866.

295 M iii. **John WHITE** was born[105] 1869.

296 F iv. **Mary Jane WHITE** was born[105] 1872.

297 M v. **Edward C WHITE** was born[105] 1877.

99. **Martha Jane WEED** (Silas Gardner, Samuel, Samuel, John, John, Jonas) was born[106] 12 Jan 1824 in New York. She died[107] 7 May 1858 in Brooklyn, Kings, NY and was buried[107] in Green-Wood Cemetery, Brooklyn, NY.

---

[104]1880 Federal census, Wappinger, Dutchess, NY Dis 72.
[105]1880 Federal census, Newburgh, Orange, NY.
[106]1850 Federal Census, Brooklyn, Kings, NY Ward 11.
[107]Records of Green-Wood cemetery, Brooklyn, NY.

Martha married[108] **William Benjamin BOOZ** on 26 Jul 1843 in Brooklyn, Kings, NY.

They had the following children:

    298   M   i.   **Randolph BOOZ** was born 1844. He died[107] 7 Jul 1848 in Brooklyn, Kings, NY and was buried[107] in Green-Wood Cemetery, Brooklyn, NY.

+   299   F   ii.   **Frances Amelia BOOZ** was born 10 Jan 1846 and died 8 Feb 1893.

+   300   F   iii. **Elizabeth L BOOZ** was born 8 Feb 1848.

+   301   M   iv. **Winfield Scott BOOZ** was born 1850 and died 3 Nov 1893.

100.**Robert Lockwood WEED** (Silas Gardner, Samuel, Samuel, John, John, Jonas) was born[109] 1828 in New York.

Robert married[109] **Henrietta UNKNOWN**. Henrietta was born 1826 in New Jersey.

They had the following children:

    302   F   i.   **Orlando WEED** was born[109] 1850 in New York.

    303   F   ii.   **Lauretta WEED** was born[110] 1852 in New York.

    304   F   iii. **Viola Eliza WEED** was born[110] 1857 in New York.

    305   M   iv. **Henry C WEED** was born[110] Apr 1860 in New York.

    306   M   v.   **Wigfall B WEED** was born[110] 1862 in New York.

101.**Frances M WEED** (Silas Gardner, Samuel, Samuel, John, John, Jonas) was born[111] 1831 in New York.

Frances married **William TURNBULL**. William was born[111] 1824 in Scotland. He died 13 Oct 1895.

---

[108]Brooklyn Daily Eagle, Friday, July 28, 1843.
[109]1860 Federal Census, Brooklyn, Kings, NY Ward 7 Dis 2.
[110]1880 Federal census, Jersey City, Hudson, NJ Dis 34.
[111]1850 Federal Census, Brooklyn, Kings, NY Ward 4.

They had the following children:

+   307   F   i.   **Emily TURNBULL** was born 1848.

       308   M   ii.   **John TURNBULL** was born[112] 1850 in Connecticut.

       309   F   iii.   **Julia TURNBULL** was born[112] 1858 in Maryland.

---

[112] 1870 Federal Census, Baltimore, Baltimore, MD Ward 18.

58

Eighth Generation

114.**Martha MERRITT**[1] (Mary WEED, Samuel, Nathaniel, Samuel, John, John, Jonas) was born[2] 8 Jul 1794. She died[2] 14 Sep 1848 and was buried[2] in Cedar Hill Cemetery, Newburgh, NY.

Martha married[1] **Gilbert HOLMES**[1] on 1844.

They had the following children:

+   310   F   i.   **Mary HOLMES** was born 4 Mar 1819.

+   311   F   ii.   **Charlotte HOLMES** was born 14 Apr 1822 and died 6 Aug 1886.

+   312   F   iii.   **Martha HOLMES** died 19 May 1865.

115.**Josiah MERRITT**[2] (Mary WEED, Samuel, Nathaniel, Samuel, John, John, Jonas) was born[2] 21 Aug 1796. He died[3] 23 Feb 1869.

Josiah married[2] **Catherine FOWLER**[2] on 1817.

They had the following children:

+   313   M   i.   **Caleb MERRITT** was born 1817.

116.**Daniel MERRITT** (Mary WEED, Samuel, Nathaniel, Samuel, John, John, Jonas) was born[3] 1799. He died[3] 1867 and was buried[2] in Cedar Hill Cemetery, Newburgh, NY.

Daniel married **Eliza HAIT**[3]. Eliza died[3] 1891.

They had the following children:

   314   M   i.   **Hiram MERRITT**[4].

---

[1]Frank L. Crawford, Morris D' Camp Crawford and his wife, Charlotte Holmes Crawford: their lives, ancestries and descendants, Page 34.
[2]Frank L. Crawford, Morris D' Camp Crawford and his wife, Charlotte Holmes Crawford: their lives, ancestries and descendants, Page 35.
[3]Frank L. Crawford, Morris D' Camp Crawford and his wife, Charlotte Holmes Crawford: their lives, ancestries and descendants, Page 36.
[4]Frank L. Crawford, Morris D' Camp Crawford and his wife, Charlotte Holmes Crawford: their lives,

315 M   ii.   **Daniel H MERRITT**[4].

316 M   iii. **Theodore MERRITT**[4].

317 F   iv.   **Mary Jane MERRITT**[4].

> Mary married **Daniel MCFARLANE**[4].

121.**Samuel WEED** (Samuel Kniffin, Samuel, Nathaniel, Samuel, John, John, Jonas) was born[5] 20 Feb 1813. He died[6] 13 Nov 1898 and was buried[6] in Patton Cemetery, Newburgh, NY.

Samuel married[7,8] **Jane MORRISON** on 23 Sep 1836 in Little Britain, Orange, NY. Jane was born 24 May 1817. She died 21 Aug 1878.

They had the following children:

318 F   i.   **Sarah Jane WEED** was born[9,10] 23 Aug 1838 in New York. She died[10] 5 Jun 1925 and was buried[10] in Wallkill Valley Cemetery, Walden, NY.

319 F   ii.   **Harriet Patton WEED** was born[6,9] 31 Dec 1839 in New York. She died[6,7] 4 Oct 1852 and was buried[6] in Patton Cemetery, Newburgh, NY.

+   320 M   iii. **Samuel K WEED** was born 16 Dec 1841 and died 9 Jun 1925.

122.**Charles WEED** (Samuel Kniffin, Samuel, Nathaniel, Samuel, John, John, Jonas) was born[5,11] 23 Apr 1815. He died[11,12] 23 Sep 1879 and

---

ancestries and descendants, Page 37.
[5]William Penn Vail, M.D., Moses Vail of Huntington, L.I., Page 86.
[6]Orange County, NY Genealogical Society, Records from Newburgh, New Windsor and other nearby towns.
[7]Portrait and Biographical record of Rockland and Orange Counties, Page 453.
[8]Orange County, NY Genealogical Society, Orange County Press Deaths and Marriages, 1865-1869.
[9]1850 Federal Census, New Windsor, Orange, NY.
[10]Wallkill Valley Cemetery, Walden, NY.
[11]The Historical Society of Newburgh Bay and the Highlands, Genealogical Notes of Raphael A. Weed.
[12]The Historical Society of Newburgh Bay and the Highlands, Account book and diary of Jane

was buried[10,11] in Wallkill Valley Cemetery, Walden, NY.

Charles married[8] **Elizabeth BEATTY** on 5 Oct 1837 in Little Britain, Orange, NY. Elizabeth was born[11] 20 Oct 1809. She died[11,12] 4 Nov 1869 and was buried[10,11] in Wallkill Valley Cemetery, Walden, NY.

They had the following children:

| | 321 | F | i. | **Susan J WEED** was born[11] 10 Jan 1839. She died[11] 2 Mar 1869 and was buried[11] in Wallkill Valley Cemetery, Walden, NY. |

+ 322 M ii. **Israel Beatty WEED** was born 19 Dec 1841 and died 26 Mar 1899.

323 F iii. **Nancy C WEED** was born[13] 1845 in New York.

+ 324 F iv. **Sarah E WEED** was born Oct 1848.

124.**Nathaniel WEED** (Samuel Kniffin, Samuel, Nathaniel, Samuel, John, John, Jonas) was born[5] 27 May 1819. He died[12] 11 Feb 1887.

Nathaniel married **Amanda COOLEY**. Amanda died[12] 3 Aug 1882.

They had the following children:

+ 325 M i. **Nathaniel King WEED** was born 1857 and died 31 Dec 1899.

326 F ii. **Elizabeth Amanda WEED** was born[14,15] Aug 1858 in New York.

Elizabeth married[12] **William Daniel BAGSHAW** on 24 Jun 1891. William was born[15] Aug 1856 in New York.

327 M iii. **Charles Cooley WEED** was born[16] 18 Sep 1861. He died[16] 20 Apr 1862 and was buried[16] in Little Britain Cemetery, New Windsor, NY.

328 M iv. **William E WEED** was born[14] 1863.

126.**William Roe WEED** (Samuel Kniffin, Samuel, Nathaniel, Samuel,

---

Morrison Weed.
[13]1850 Federal Census, Montgomery, Orange, NY.
[14]1870 Federal Census, New Windsor, Orange, NY.
[15]1900 Federal Census, Newburgh, Orange, NY Ward 6 Dis 43.
[16]Orange County, NY Genealogical Society, New Windsor, NY cemetery inscriptions.

John, John, Jonas) was born[5,17] 26 Feb 1825 in Coldenham, Orange, NY. He died[12,17] 8 Apr 1893 in Newburgh, Orange, NY.

William married **Elmira DOANE**, daughter of David DOANE and Jane DUNN.

They had the following children:

+   329 F   i.   **Mary L WEED** was born 1851.

+   330 M   ii.   **Charles W WEED** was born 19 Jan 1853.

+   331 F   iii.   **Elmira J WEED** was born 1856.

+   332 M   iv.   **Ashton Doane WEED** was born Nov 1859.

+   333 M   v.   **Edgar V.K. WEED** was born 1861 and died 16 Dec 1893.

138. **Abby Jane MILBURN** (Hester MARONEY, Elizabeth WEED, Samuel, Samuel, John, John, Jonas) was born[18] 4 Nov 1830. She died[18] 23 Feb 1916 and was buried[18] in Gardnertown Cemetery, Newburgh, NY.

Abby married[19] **Carpenter STANTON** on 1 Nov 1855 in Newburgh, Orange, NY. Carpenter was born 17 Feb 1830. He died 22 Aug 1896 and was buried in Gardnertown Cemetery, Newburgh, NY.

They had the following children:

+   334 M   i.   **Peter Cole STANTON** was born 4 Sep 1857 and died 8 Mar 1913.

139. **Samuel J MILBURN** (Hester MARONEY, Elizabeth WEED, Samuel, Samuel, John, John, Jonas) was born[20] Apr 1835.

Samuel married[21] **Maria E UNKNOWN**.

They had the following children:

    335 F   i.   **Lilia L MILBURN** was born[21] 1862.

---

[17]Portrait and Biographical record of Rockland and Orange Counties, Page 163, 164.
[18]Gardnertown Cemetery, Newburgh, NY.
[19]Gardnertown UMC, Newburgh, NY Record of Marriages.
[20]1900 Federal Census, Newburgh, Orange, NY Dis 46.
[21]1880 Federal census, Newburgh, Orange, NY.

336 F   ii. **Orvilla MILBURN** was born[21] 1868.

+   337 M   iii. **Vaness T MILBURN** was born Sep 1869.

338 M   iv. **Lewis Samuel MILBURN** was born[21] 1871. He died 1944 and was buried[18] in Gardnertown Cemetery, Newburgh, NY.

Lewis married **Anna F CRAWFORD**. Anna was born 1876. She died 1944 and was buried[18] in Gardnertown Cemetery, Newburgh, NY.

339 M   v. **Alva B MILBURN** was born[20,21] Jun 1873.

Alva married[22] (1) **Elena UNKNOWN**.

Alva also married (2) **Nettie WAITE**. Nettie was born[6] 28 Apr 1879. She died[6] 28 Oct 1898 and was buried[6] in Gardnertown Cemetery, Newburgh, NY.

340 F   vi. **Cora Hester MILBURN** was born[20,21] 23 Jun 1877. She died 19 Sep 1916 and was buried[18] in Gardnertown Cemetery, Newburgh, NY.

Cora married **Lawrence S SPARKES**. Lawrence was born 24 Jun 1877. He died 24 Jul 1914 and was buried[18] in Gardnertown Cemetery, Newburgh, NY.

142. **Martha MILBURN** (Hester MARONEY, Elizabeth WEED, Samuel, Samuel, John, John, Jonas) was born[23] 1843.

Martha married **Unknown SHAY**.

They had the following children:

341 F   i. **Adele SHAY** was born[24] 1863 in New York.

143. **Margaret Ann MILBURN** (Hester MARONEY, Elizabeth WEED, Samuel, Samuel, John, John, Jonas) was born 1847. She died 1911 and was buried[18] in Gardnertown Cemetery, Newburgh, NY.

Margaret married **Halsey W BROWN**. Halsey was born 1850. He

---

[22] 1910 Federal Census, Newburgh, Orange, NY Ward 6 Dis 62.
[23] 1860 Federal Census, Newburgh, Orange, NY.
[24] 1870 Federal Census, Newburgh, Orange, NY, Ward 1.

was buried[18] in Gardnertown Cemetery, Newburgh, NY.

They had the following children:

   342   F   i. **Elenora BROWN** was born[21] 1878.

   343   M   ii. **Henry H BROWN** was born[21,25] May 1879.

   344   F   iii. **Sally May BROWN** was born[25] Aug 1881.

   345   F   iv. **Mattie V BROWN** was born[25] Jun 1886.

   346   M   v. **Charles D BROWN** was born 20 Jun 1888. He died 26 Jun 1888 and was buried[18] in Gardnertown Cemetery, Newburgh, NY.

146. **George MARONEY** (Uriah MARONEY, Elizabeth WEED, Samuel, Samuel, John, John, Jonas) was born[26] 1844 in New York.

George married[27] **Margaret UNKNOWN**.

They had the following children:

   347   M   i. **Willie MARONEY** was born[28] 1871 in New York.

   348   M   ii. **Edward MARONEY** was born[28] 1872 in New York.

151. **Sarah Elizabeth MARONEY** (Uriah MARONEY, Elizabeth WEED, Samuel, Samuel, John, John, Jonas) was born[29,30] Apr 1856 in New York.

Sarah married **Frank HENNION**. Frank was born[30] Apr 1844 in New Jersey.

They had the following children:

   349   M   i. **Richard B HENNION** was born[30] Jun 1883 in New York.

---

[25]1900 Federal Census, Newburgh, Orange, NY Ward 6 Dis 44.
[26]1850 Federal Census, Ramapo, Rockland, NY.
[27]1880 Federal census, Nyack, Rockland, NY Dis 55.
[28]1880 Federal census, Nyack, Rockland, NY Dis 55.
[29]1860 Federal Census, Ramapo, Rockland, NY.
[30]1900 Federal Census, Brooklyn, Kings, NY Ward 23 Dis 387.

+ 350 M ii. **Frank Walter HENNION** was born 24 Feb 1885.

351 M iii. **Jay O HENNION** was born[30] Aug 1891 in New York.

152.**Nathan MARONEY** (Uriah MARONEY, Elizabeth WEED, Samuel, Samuel, John, John, Jonas) was born[29] 1858 in New York.

Nathan married[31] **Minnie SCOTT**. Minnie was born[31] Mar 1857 in New York.

They had the following children:

352 F i. **Sarah MARONEY** was born[31] Mar 1888 in New York.

153.**Sarah Ann WEED** (Charles, Samuel, Samuel, Samuel, John, John, Jonas) was born 1830 in Pleasant Valley, Sullivan, NY. She died[32] 1 Sep 1889 in Middletown, Orange, NY and was buried[32] in Hillside Cemetery, Middletown, NY.

Sarah married[33] **John L SCOTT**, son of Thaddeus SCOTT, on 16 Dec 1852. John was born[33] 21 Oct 1826 in Burlingham, Sullivan, NY. He died[33] 8 Feb 1917 in Middletown, Orange, NY and was buried[33] in Hillside Cemetery, Middletown, NY.

They had the following children:

+ 353 M i. **Charles Weed SCOTT** was born Oct 1853.

354 F ii. **Henrietta SCOTT**[34] was born 1855.

Henrietta married[32] **Unknown DAVY**.

+ 355 M iii. **George Swalm SCOTT** was born 12 Feb 1856 and died 18 Mar 1932.

356 M iv. **Frank SCOTT** was born Aug 1870. He died[35] 26 Jul 1871.

---

[31] 1900 Federal Census, Ramapo, Rockland, NY Dis 73.
[32] Middletown Daily Press, Tuesday, September 3 1889.
[33] Middletown Times Press, Friday, February 9, 1917.
[34] 1860 Federal Census, Wallkill, Orange, NY.
[35] Middletown Evening Press, Thursday, July 27 1871.

156.**John Hollister WEED** (Charles, Samuel, Samuel, Samuel, John, John, Jonas) was born[36] 6 May 1837 in Town Of Crawford, Orange, NY. He died[36] 22 Aug 1921 in Allentown, PA and was buried[37] in Hillside Cemetery, Middletown, NY.

John married[38] **Mary Ann SHARP**. Mary was born 14 Dec 1842. She died 10 Aug 1915 and was buried in Hillside Cemetery, Middletown, NY.

They had the following children:

    357 M   i. **Henry Thomas WEED** was born 14 Sep 1863 in Bloomingburg, Sullivan, NY. He died[39] 16 Apr 1905 in Chicago, Cook, IL.

+ 358 M ii. **William Sharp WEED** was born 25 Feb 1866 and died 20 Nov 1954.

+ 359 M iii. **Elliott WEED** was born 20 Jun 1868.

    360 M iv. **Frank Odell WEED** was born 27 Jul 1873 in Pine Bush, Orange, NY. He died[40] 22 Apr 1905 in Middletown, Orange, NY.

               Frank married[41] **Myrtie CUMMIMGS** on 22 Jan 1899 in Walden, Orange, NY.

+ 361 M v. **J Spencer WEED** was born 24 Dec 1879 and died 11 Nov 1969.

157.**Mary E WEED** (Charles, Samuel, Samuel, Samuel, John, John, Jonas) was born Sep 1840. She died[42] 10 Jan 1908 in Bloomfield, Essex, NJ and was buried[42] in Bloomfield Cemetery, Bloomfield, NJ.

---

[36]Middletown Times Press, Tuesday, August 23, 1921.
[37]Hillside Cemetery, Middletown, NY.
[38]Orange County, NY Genealogical Society, Notes of Elizabeth Horton.
[39]Middletown Daily Times, Monday, April 17 1905.
[40]Middletown Daily Times, Monday, April 24 1905.
[41]Orange County, NY Genealogical Society, Marriage Notices from the Goshen Independent Republican.
[42]Letter from Bloomfield Cemetery Co, 383 Belleville Ave, Bloomfield NJ 07003.

Mary married[43] **Hiram V PECK,** son of Prosper PECK and Rebecca VAN AMBURGH. Hiram was born 1837. He died[42] 28 Dec 1904 in Bloomfield, Essex, NJ and was buried[42] in Bloomfield Cemetery, Bloomfield, NJ.

They had the following children:

    362   M   i.   **Emory M PECK** was born[44] 19 Sep 1861 in Boonton, Morris, NJ. He died[44] 23 Nov 1933 in Bloomfield, Essex, NJ and was buried[44] in Pompton Plains, Passaic, NJ.

                      Emory married[38] **Elizabeth PINE.**

158.**Jane DuBois WEED** (Charles, Samuel, Samuel, Samuel, John, John, Jonas) was born[45] 13 Jan 1845. She died[45] 26 Nov 1869 and was buried[45] in Bloomingburg Rural Cemetery, Bloomingburg, NY.

Jane married[43] **Increase IVORY**, son of James IVORY and Margaret UNKNOWN, on 30 Jan 1861 in Bloomingburg, Sullivan, NY. Increase was buried in Bloomingburg Cemetery, Bloomingburg, NY.

They had the following children:

    363   M   i.   **Warren O IVORY** was born[46] 10 Nov 1863 in Pleasant Valley, Sullivan, NY. He died[47] 18 Jun 1945 in Goshen, Orange, NY and was buried[48] in Bloomingburg Rural Cemetery, Bloomingburg, NY.

                      Warren married[41] **Arcie UNKNOWN** on 1891.

160.**John Floyd WEED** (Samuel B, Samuel, Samuel, Samuel, John, John, Jonas) was born[49] 4 Sep 1839 in Phillipsport, Sullivan, NY. He

---

[43]Methodist Episcopal Church of Bloomingburg, NY records of Marriages.
[44]State of New Jersey death certificate.
[45]Bloomingburg Cemetery, Bloomingburg, NY.
[46]1900 Federal Census, Wallkill, Orange, NY.
[47]Record of Deaths at the Orange Co., NY Home and Infirmary., Orange County Genealogical Society, Goshen, NY.
[48]Middletown Times Herald, Tuesday, June 19, 1945.
[49]1900 Federal Census, Rochester, Monroe, NY Dist 120.

died[50] 1 May 1909 in Rochester, Monroe, NY and was buried[51] in Mt. Hope Cemetery, Rochester, NY.

John married[50] **Irena Jane LUDINGTON**, daughter of William S LUDINGTON and Irena MASTEN, on 30 May 1865 in Phillipsport, Sullivan, NY. Irena was born[50] 16 Oct 1845 in Phillipsport, Sullivan, NY. She died[50] 5 Nov 1921 in Rochester, Monroe, NY.

        Married by Rev. Isaac H. Lunt

John and Irena had the following children:

364	F	i.	**Orvilla WEED** was born[52,53] 3 Sep 1866 in Phillipsport, Sullivan, NY. She died[53] 4 Nov 1886 in Warsaw, Wyoming, NY and was buried[54] in Warsaw Cemetery, Warsaw, NY.
365	F	ii.	**Blanche E WEED** was born[49,50] 21 Jul 1871 in Titusville, Crawford, PA.
+ 366	M	iii.	**Guy L WEED** was born 17 Mar 1874 and died 8 Aug 1907.
367	F	iv.	**Olive Maud WEED** was born[49,50] 21 May 1877 in Buffalo, Erie, NY.
368	M	v.	**Roy WEED** was born[52] 1879 in New York.
369	F	vi.	**Lora Bell WEED** was born[49,50] 28 Jul 1880 in Warsaw, Wyoming, NY. Lora married[55] **Lester BUREN** on 1 Sep 1902 in Rochester, Monroe, NY.
370	M	vii.	**Frederick L WEED** was born[49,50] 7 Jul 1883 in Warsaw, Wyoming, NY.

---

[50]Civil War pension file of John F. Weed.
[51]Office of Vital Records, County of Monroe, Rochester, NY.
[52]1880 Federal census, Warsaw, Wyoming, NY Dist 211.
[53]Town of Warsaw, Wyoming, NY Vital Records.
[54]Rootsweb.com, Wyoming County, NY cemetery records.
[55]City of Rochester, NY Archives and records center. Historic Marriage records research site.
.

162. **William Thair WEED**[56] (Samuel B, Samuel, Samuel, Samuel, John, John, Jonas) was born 1846 in Phillipsport, Sullivan, NY. He died between 1875-1880 in Liberty, Sullivan, NY.

William married[38] **Mary GARRETT**. Mary was born[57] Nov 1851 in Liberty, Sullivan, NY. She died[58] 26 Jan 1907 in Liberty, Sullivan, NY.

They had the following children:

    371 F   i.   **Eva WEED** was born[57] Oct 1875 in Liberty, Sullivan, NY.

                      Eva married **Frank RAY**.

163. **Ermon Romain WEED** (Samuel B, Samuel, Samuel, Samuel, John, John, Jonas) was born[51,59] 16 Nov 1848 in Phillipsport, Sullivan, NY. He died[51] 6 Jul 1921 in Rochester, Monroe, NY and was buried[51,60] in Fairview Cemetery, Beacon, NY.

Ermon married[61] **Mary Elizabeth PENDLETON** on 15 Apr 1874 in Matteawan, Dutchess, NY. Mary was born[59] 2 Apr 1849. She died 9 May 1908 and was buried[62] in Fairview Cemetery, Beacon, NY.

```
Married by Rev J.L. Scott
```

Ermon and Mary had the following children:

+   372 F   i.   **Inez A WEED** was born 8 Dec 1875 and died 16 Mar 1920.

    373 F   ii. **Leola Della WEED** was born[59] 21 Nov 1879. She died 22 Oct 1962 and was buried[62] in Fairview Cemetery, Beacon, NY.

    374 F   iii. **Mary E WEED** "Mamie" was born[59] 17 Jan 1882. She died 26 Mar 1951 and was buried[62]

---

[56] 1850 Federal Census, Mamakating, Sullivan, NY.
[57] 1900 Federal Census, Liberty, Sullivan, NY Dist 92.
[58] Village of Liberty, NY vital records.
[59] 1900 Federal Census, Matteawan, Dutchess, NY Dist 10.
[60] The Fishkill Standard, Saturday, July 9, 1921.
[61] The Fishkill Standard, Saturday, April 18, 1874.
[62] Fairview Cemetery, Beacon, NY.

in Fairview Cemetery, Beacon, NY.

375 F   iv. **Daisy L WEED** was born[59] 30 Nov 1884. She died 15 Apr 1948 and was buried[62] in Fairview Cemetery, Beacon, NY.

Daisy married **Frank Creighton SHAW**. Frank was born 29 Jan 1874. He died 29 May 1935 and was buried[62] in Fairview Cemetery, Beacon, NY.

376 M   v. **Lewis E WEED** was born[59] 18 Apr 1891. He died 17 Aug 1947 and was buried[63] in Hillside Cemetery, Clarendon, Orleans, NY.

Lewis married[64] **Edna M MCCRILLIS**. Edna was born 1891. She died 17 Sep 1975 and was buried[63] in Hillside Cemetery, Clarendon, Orleans, NY.

164.**Mary R WEED** (Samuel B, Samuel, Samuel, Samuel, John, John, Jonas) was born[49,51] 7 May 1851 in Phillipsport, Sullivan, NY. She died[51] 26 Jun 1926 in Rochester, Monroe, NY and was buried[65] 28 Jun 1926 in Mt. Hope Cemetery, Rochester, NY.

Mary married **Ira M LUDINGTON**, son of William S LUDINGTON and Irena MASTEN. Ira was born[50,51,56] 3 Apr 1849 in Phillipsport, Sullivan, NY. He died[51] 27 Jan 1910 in Rochester, Monroe, NY and was buried[65] 29 Jan 1910 in Mt. Hope Cemetery, Rochester, NY.

They had the following children:

+   377 M   i. **Claude LUDINGTON** was born 25 Dec 1875 and died 2 Feb 1934.

+   378 F   ii. **Mabel C LUDINGTON** was born 1876 and was buried 8 May 1934.

379 M   iii. **Ira M LUDINGTON JR** was born[49] 5 Nov 1878 in Rochester, Monroe, NY. He died 1924 in Easton, Washington, NY.

---

[63]USgenweb.org, cemetery records of Orleans County, NY.
[64]1920 Federal Census, Murray, Orleans, NY Dist 226.
[65]Records of the Mt. Hope cemetery, Rochester, NY.

Ira married **Pearl Amelia RICE** on 11 Nov 1902 in Greenwich, Washington, NY. Pearl was born 7 Aug 1882 in Easton, Washington, NY. She died 20 Oct 1964 in Albany, Albany, NY.

380 M   iv.   **Earl LUDINGTON** was born Nov 1880. He was buried[65] 8 Aug 1884 in Mt. Hope Cemetery, Rochester, NY.

166. **Delaphine WEED** (Samuel B, Samuel, Samuel, Samuel, John, John, Jonas) was born[59] 3 Mar 1860 in Phillipsport, Sullivan, NY. She died[66] 18 Aug 1950 in Poughkeepsie, Dutchess, NY and was buried[66] in Poughkeepsie Rural Cemetery, Poughkeepsie, NY.

Delaphine married[38] **Frederick REICK JR**. Frederick was born[59] Aug 1857. He died[66] Dec 1945.

They had the following children:

+   381 F   i.   **Sadie M REICK** was born Dec 1883 and died Feb 1920.

+   382 F   ii.   **Esther J REICK** was born 30 Nov 1896 and died 20 Nov 1989.

     383 M   iii.   **Gerald REICK** was born[59] Aug 1899 in New York. He died[66] 1944.

                   Gerald married[67] **Bertha DEYO**.

169. **Mary Josephine EVENS** (Jane WEED, Samuel, Samuel, Samuel, John, John, Jonas) was born[68] 16 Sep 1848. She died[69] 8 Aug 1930 in Pine Bush, Orange, NY and was buried[70] in New Prospect Cemetery, Pine Bush, NY.

Mary married **John Thomas MARKS**. John was born May 1853 and was baptized[71] 3 Dec 1886 in New Prospect Church, Pine Bush, NY. He died[71] 28 Jul 1924 and was buried[70] in New Prospect

---

[66]Poughkeepsie New Yorker, Friday, August 18, 1950.
[67]Interview with Nancy Bauer Hoolihan.
[68]Interview with Jerome M. Nathan, 5 Feb 2004.
[69]Middletown Times Herald, Wednesday, August 13 1930.
[70]New Prospect Cemetery, Pine Bush, NY.
[71]New Prospect Church, Pine Bush, NY Church records.

Cemetery, Pine Bush, NY.

They had the following children:

384   F   i.   **Viola A MARKS** "Vicky" was born Oct 1877 and was baptized[71] 3 Mar 1894 in New Prospect Church, Pine Bush, NY. She died[68,72] 17 Feb 1962 in Kingston, Ulster, NY and was buried[70] in New Prospect Cemetery, Pine Bush, NY.

+   385   F   ii.   **Elsie Jane MARKS** was born Dec 1878 and died 13 Nov 1934.

386   F   iii.   **Edith M MARKS** was born Jul 1883 and was baptized[71] 2 Sep 1887 in New Prospect Church, Pine Bush, NY. She died[73] 27 Jan 1957 in Kingston, Ulster, NY and was buried[70] in New Prospect Cemetery, Pine Bush, NY.

Edith married[71] **Fred KAIN** on 12 Aug 1911 in New Prospect Church, Pine Bush, NY. Fred was buried[70] in New Prospect Cemetery, Pine Bush, NY.

387   F   iv.   **Pearl F MARKS** was born Jun 1886 and was baptized[71] 2 Sep 1887 in New Prospect Church, Pine Bush, NY. She died[74,75] 1 Nov 1963 in Kingston, Ulster, NY and was buried[70] in New Prospect Cemetery, Pine Bush, NY.

Pearl married[76] **Frederick E LOBDELL**. Frederick was buried[70] in New Prospect Cemetery, Pine Bush, NY.

---

[72]Kingston Daily Freeman, Monday, February 19, 1962.
[73]Kingston Daily Freeman, Wednesday, January 30, 1957.
[74]Times Herald Record, Saturday, November 2 1963.
[75]Kingston Daily Freeman, Friday, November 1, 1963.
[76]1930 Federal Census, Town of Shawangunk, Ulster County, NY.

176. **Cynthia M WOODEN**[77] (Harriet WEED, Samuel, Samuel, Samuel, John, John, Jonas) was born[78] Jul 1849 in Michigan.

Cynthia married[79] **Joseph POPP**. Joseph was born[78] Dec 1846 in Germany.

They had the following children:

    388   M   i.   **William J POPP**[80] was born[78] Oct 1884 in Ohio.

187. **Annie Florilla WEED** (John, Samuel, Samuel, Samuel, John, John, Jonas) was born[81] 8 Dec 1860 in Villenova, Chautauqua, NY. She died[82] 17 Feb 1905 in Chicago, Cook, IL and was buried in Villenova Cemetery, Balcom, NY.

Annie married[81] **John WOODWORTH** on 3 Mar 1890.

They had the following children:

    389   i.   **Leslie Dale WOODWORTH**.

191. **Myrtie Delia WEED** "Mertie" (John, Samuel, Samuel, Samuel, John, John, Jonas) was born[81] 18 Oct 1868 in Cherry Creek, Chautauqua, NY. She died 14 Jan 1939 in Cherry Creek, Chautauqua, NY and was buried[83] in Highland Cemetery, Cherry Creek, NY.

Mertie married[84] **Berlin P CRUMB**. Berlin was born 28 Sep 1874. He died[84] 23 Oct 1938 in Cherry Creek, Chautauqua, NY and was buried[83] in Highland Cemetery, Cherry Creek, NY.

They had the following children:

---

[77]1860 Federal Census, Hillsdale, MI.
[78]1900 Federal Census, Toledo, Lucas, OH Dis 91.
[79]Toledo Daily Blade, Tuesday, September 21, 1909.
[80]1920 Federal Census, Toledo, Lucas, OH Dist 76.
[81]Manuscript of David E Moon - Record of Moon, Pierce, Arnold and Holt families. Circa 1930. In possession of Patty Mallory, Houston, TX.
[82]State of Illinois Online Death records, www.cyberdriveillinois.com.
[83]USgenweb.org, Cemetery records of Cherry Creek, NY.
[84]Letter from Joyce Chase, Town Historian, Cherry Creek, NY.

390　F　　i.　**Ilene B CRUMB**[85] was born 1901. She was buried[86] in Highland Cemetery, Cherry Creek, NY.

+　391　F　　ii.　**Mildred Marie CRUMB** was born 11 Sep 1902 and died Apr 1992.

+　392　F　　iii.　**Albertine F CRUMB** was born 1903.

+　393　M　　iv.　**Dale Gerald CRUMB** was born 4 Apr 1908 and died Jan 1986.

+　394　F　　v.　**Gladys Elsie CRUMB** was born 6 Mar 1909 and died 10 Dec 1934.

193. **Herbert Odell WEED** (John, Samuel, Samuel, Samuel, John, John, Jonas) was born[87] 7 Jan 1874 in Cherry Creek, Chautauqua, NY. He died[88] 3 May 1942 in Cherry Creek, Chautauqua, NY and was buried[89] in Highland Cemetery, Cherry Creek, NY.

Herbert married[87] **Mattie Maude WEAVER** on 9 May 1905. Mattie was born[87] 22 Mar 1875.

They had the following children:

+　395　F　　i.　**Marjory Harriet WEED** was born 26 Oct 1915.

195. **James Marshall WEED** (Levi, Samuel, Samuel, Samuel, John, John, Jonas) was born[90] 6 Jul 1857 in Walker Valley, Ulster, NY. He died 19 Feb 1926 in Pine Bush, Orange, NY and was buried[91] in Walker Valley Cemetery, Walker Valley, NY.

---

[85]1910 Federal Census, Cherry Creek, Chautauqua, NY Dis 112.
[86]Interview with Madolyn Cummings, September 30, 2005.
[87]Email from Bob Weaver.
[88]Email from Sylvia Higbee Bailey.
[89]Rootsweb.com, Chautauqua County, NY cemetery records.
[90]James Marshall Weed Family Bible.
[91]Walker Valley, NY cemetery records.

James Marshall Weed

James married[90] **Mary Isabella BAKER,** daughter of Justus BAKER and Nancy C CRAWFORD, on 25 Jul 1883 in Walker Valley, Ulster, NY. Mary was born[90] 7 Jul 1859 in Walker Valley, Ulster, NY. She died 11 Dec 1937 in New York, New York, NY and was buried[92] in Walker Valley Cemetery, Walker Valley, NY.

They had the following children:

+   396   M   i.   **William Lloyd Garrison WEED** was born 17 Jul 1884 and died 25 Aug 1954.

+   397   M   ii.   **Lewis Horton WEED** was born 4 Jul 1887 and died 10 May 1968.

+   398   M   iii.   **Reubin Watson WEED** was born 8 Jul 1890 and died 24 Nov 1957.

+   399   F   iv.   **Mabel Elsie WEED** was born 10 Feb 1898 and died 26 Dec 1962.

    400   F   v.   **Elizabeth Isabella WEED** "Betty" was born[90] 31 Mar 1901. She died[93] 26 Jul 1987.

                 Betty married[90] **Robert Hilliard GLEASON.**

196.**George E WEED** (Levi, Samuel, Samuel, Samuel, John, John,

---

[92]Walker Valley, NY Cemetery.
[93]Social Security Death Index.

Jonas) was born[94] 15 Mar 1860 in Walker Valley, Ulster, NY and was baptized[95] 7 Dec 1890 in Walker Valley, Ulster, NY. He died[96] 13 Aug 1926 in Middletown, Orange, NY and was buried[91] in Walker Valley Cemetery, Walker Valley, NY.

George married[97] **Maria Jane LAFORGE**, daughter of Isaac LAFORGE and Ellen H SATTERLEY, on 1 Nov 1891 in Walker Valley, Ulster, NY. The marriage ended in divorce. Maria was born[98] 28 Jan 1870 in Crawford, Ulster, NY. She died[99] 24 Mar 1947 in Newburgh, Orange, NY and was buried[99] in Wallkill Cemetery, Walden, NY.

They had the following children:

    401 F   i. **Nellafornia WEED** was born[93,100] 12 Oct 1892 in Walker Valley, Ulster, NY. She died[93] Aug 1987 in Goshen, Orange, NY.

+   402 M   ii. **Harry Marvon WEED** was born 26 Dec 1894 and died 14 Nov 1976.

197.**Ida Jane WEED** (Levi, Samuel, Samuel, Samuel, John, John, Jonas) was born[94] 1 Nov 1862 in Walker Valley, Ulster, NY. She died 15 Sep 1934 in Bloomingburg, Sullivan, NY and was buried in Bloomingburg Rural Cemetery, Bloomingburg, NY.

---

[94]Ida Jane Weed Gibbs Family Bible.
[95]Walker Valley, NY United Methodist Church records.
[96]The Daily Herald, Saturday, August 14 1926.
[97]Marriage Notices from the Goshen Independent Republican, Orange county genealogical society, Goshen, NY.
[98]Email from William Meredith.
[99]New York state death certificate.
[100]Social Security Application, Application of Nellafornia Weed.

Abram and Ida Weed Gibbs

Ida married **Abram L GIBBS**, son of John GIBBS and Mary CRAWFORD, on 9 Jul 1883. Abram was born[94,101] 17 Sep 1864 in Pleasant Valley, Sullivan, NY. He died[94,101] 11 Oct 1946 in Bloomingburg, Sullivan, NY and was buried in Bloomingburg Rural Cemetery, Bloomingburg, NY.

They had the following children:

403   F   i.   **Nettie Weed GIBBS** was born[102] 7 Oct 1884 in Walker Valley, Ulster, NY. She died[102] 6 Jan 1960.

                         Nettie married[102] **Robert KIRKWOOD** on 1 Sep 1915. Robert died[102] 11 Jun 1940.

+   404   F   ii.   **Mary GIBBS** was born 29 Aug 1887 and died 19 Sep 1941.

405   F   iii.   **Addie GIBBS** was born[102,103] 8 May 1889 in Walker Valley, Ulster, NY. She died[102,103] 17 Jun 1917 in High View, Sullivan, NY.

---

[101]Middletown Times Herald, Saturday, October 12, 1946.
[102]Interview with Anna Jean Allen Hilliker.
[103]Middletown Times Press, Monday, June 18, 1917.

Addie married[102] **William BARRETT** on 28
Oct 1909.

+   406   F   iv.   **Anna V GIBBS** was born 19 Jun 1895 and died
24 Jun 1987.

   407   F   v.   **Florence GIBBS** was born[102] 13 Apr 1899. She
died[102] 6 Jun 1936.

Florence married[102] **Edward POWELL** on
Nov 1928.

   408   F   vi.   **Mildred Naomi GIBBS** was born[102] 28 Apr
1904. She died[102] 14 Dec 1928 and was buried
in Bloomingburg Cemetery, Bloomingburg,
NY.

+   409   F   vii.   **Alice B GIBBS** was born 5 Nov 1905 and died
Nov 1964.

207. **Charles Wesley MILBURN**[104] (Isaac G MILBURN, Sarah WEED,
Samuel, Samuel, John, John, Jonas) was born 1834.

Charles married[104] **Phebe Jane EGGLETON** on 19 Nov 1857.
Phebe was born 4 Nov 1833. She died 3 Apr 1909 in Haverstraw,
Rockland, NY and was buried[105] in Mt. Repose Cemetery,
Haverstraw, NY.

They had the following children:

   410   F   i.   **Henrietta MILBURN** was born[106] 27 May 1858.

Henrietta married **Charles R LANE** on 19
Nov 1878.

   411   F   ii.   **Sophie Elizabeth MILBURN** was born[106] 12
May 1860.

Sophie married **George Minor BARNHART**
on 29 May 1889 in Haverstraw, Rockland,
NY. George was born 29 May 1846 in
Marlboro, Ulster, NY.

   412   M   iii.   **Daniel D MILBURN** was born[107,108] 6 Apr 1862.

---

[104]Newburgh Bay and Hudson Highlands, Records from
Newburgh, New Windsor and other nearby towns, Vol
1.
[105]Rootsweb.com, Rockland County, NY cemetery
records.
[106]1870 Federal Census, Warren, Rockland, NY.

He died 30 Aug 1916 in Haverstraw, Rockland, NY and was buried[105] in Mt. Repose Cemetery, Haverstraw, NY.

Daniel married **Catherine Lucretia BOYER** on 30 Oct 1894. Catherine was born[108] Oct 1862 in Pennsylvania.

413   M   iv.   **Wesley I MILBURN** was born[107] 1 Feb 1864. He died 14 May 1891 in Haverstraw, Rockland, NY and was buried[105] in Mt. Repose Cemetery, Haverstraw, NY.

212. **Adaline ROBERTS** (Lavinia WEED, Gardner, Samuel, Samuel, John, John, Jonas) was born[109] 1836 in New York. She died[110] 12 Nov 1872 in New Orleans, Orleans, LA and was buried[110] in Poughkeepsie Rural Cemetery, Poughkeepsie, NY.

Adaline married (1) **Frederick A EMIGH**. Frederick was born[110] 13 Dec 1829. He died[110] 6 Apr 1863 in Poughkeepsie, Dutchess, NY and was buried[110] in Poughkeepsie Rural Cemetery, Poughkeepsie, NY.

Adaline also married (2) **Unknown PENNIMAN**.

They had the following children:

414   M   i.   **Harry PENNIMAN** was born[111] 1865 in New York.

213. **Benjamin ROBERTS** (Lavinia WEED, Gardner, Samuel, Samuel, John, John, Jonas) was born[112] 1838.

Benjamin married **Caroline HOBBS**[113].

They had the following children:

+   415   M   i.   **Warren Silas ROBERTS** was born 28 Jan 1888.

---

[107]1880 Federal census, Haverstraw, Rockland, NY.
[108]1900 Federal Census, Haverstraw, Rockland, NY.
[109]1850 Federal Census, Poughkeepsie, Dutchess, NY.
[110]Records of Poughkeepsie Rural Cemetery, Poughkeepsie, NY.
[111]1870 Federal Census, Poughkeepsie, Dutchess, NY Ward 4.
[112]1860 Federal Census, Poughkeepsie, Dutchess, NY Ward 3.
[113]Email from Kurt Sobina.

+ 416 M ii. **William Henry ROBERTS** was born 1892.

417 M iii. **John ROBERTS**[113] was born in New York, New York, NY.

418 F iv. **Delia ROBERTS**[113] was born in New York, New York, NY.

419 F v. **Caroline ROBERTS**[113] was born in New York, New York, NY.

214. **Sarah R ROBERTS** (Lavinia WEED, Gardner, Samuel, Samuel, John, John, Jonas) was born[109,114] Apr 1841 in New York.

Sarah married (1) **Unknown HEWITT**.

They had the following children:

420 M i. **Walter O HEWITT** was born[112] 1858 in Wisconsin.

Sarah also married (2) **Unknown ROBINSON**[114].

216. **John J ROBERTS** (Lavinia WEED, Gardner, Samuel, Samuel, John, John, Jonas) was born 1846. He died[110] 13 Apr 1912 in Brooklyn, Kings, NY and was buried[110] in Poughkeepsie Rural Cemetery, Poughkeepsie, NY.

John married (1) **Henrietta STEWART**. Henrietta was born 1839. She died[110] 10 Oct 1870 in New York, New York, NY and was buried[110] in Poughkeepsie Rural Cemetery, Poughkeepsie, NY.

John also married (2) **Louise HUNTER**. Louise was born[110,115] 29 Dec 1870 in Brooklyn, Kings, NY. She died[110] 31 May 1960 in Kingston, Ulster, NY and was buried[110] in Poughkeepsie Rural Cemetery, Poughkeepsie, NY.

They had the following children:

+ 421 M i. **Milton N ROBERTS** was born 1889 and died 12 Mar 1979.

422 F ii. **Lavinia ROBERTS** was born[116] 1893 in New York.

423 M iii. **John ROBERTS** was born[116] 1895 in New York.

---

[114] 1900 Federal Census, Washington, Washington, DC Dis 18.
[115] City of Poughkeepsie, NY Vital records.
[116] 1910 Federal Census, Poughkeepsie, Dutchess, NY Ward 4 Dis 68.

424 M iv. **Harry ROBERTS** was born[116] 1898 in New York.

425 M v. **Walter ROBERTS** was born[116] 1902 in New York.

426 M vi. **Arthur ROBERTS** was born[110] 4 Jun 1903. He died[110] 15 Apr 1908 in Poughkeepsie, Dutchess, NY and was buried[110] in Poughkeepsie Rural Cemetery, Poughkeepsie, NY.

427 F vii. **Martha ROBERTS** was born[116] 1905 in New York.

428 M viii. **James ROBERTS** was born[116] Jan 1910 in New York.

429 F ix. **Jane ROBERTS** was born[115] 19 Jan 1910. She died[115] 3 Mar 1910 in Poughkeepsie, Dutchess, NY and was buried[110] in Poughkeepsie Rural Cemetery, Poughkeepsie, NY.

218. **Phebe Ann ROBERTS** (Lavinia WEED, Gardner, Samuel, Samuel, John, John, Jonas) was born[112,114] Sep 1850 in New York. She died between 1920-1930.

Phebe married[117] **Charles T JOHNSON**. Charles was born[114] Jun 1843 in New York.

They had the following children:

430 F i. **Clara JOHNSON** was born[118] 1871 in New York.

431 M ii. **Samuel Hooper JOHNSON** was born[110] 26 May 1873. He died[110] 7 Jun 1874 in Washington, Washington, DC and was buried[110] in Poughkeepsie Rural Cemetery, Poughkeepsie, NY.

---

[117]Edward O. Bartlett, The Dutchess County Regiment: (150th Regiment of NY state Volunteer Infantry) in the Civil War, its story told by its members, Danbury, CT, Danbury Medical Print Co., 1907, Page 289.
[118]1880 Federal census, Washington, Washington, DC Dis 58.

432 F iii. **Sarah JOHNSON** died[110] 5 Aug 1876 in Washington, Washington, DC and was buried[110] in Poughkeepsie Rural Cemetery, Poughkeepsie, NY.

433 M iv. **Charles T JOHNSON** was born[114] Nov 1877 in Washington, Washington, DC.

434 F v. **Lizzie M JOHNSON** was born Jan 1879. She died[110] 24 Jul 1879 in Washington, Washington, DC and was buried[110] in Poughkeepsie Rural Cemetery, Poughkeepsie, NY.

435 F vi. **Lillie JOHNSON** was born Apr 1880. She died[110] 8 Sep 1880 in Washington, Washington, DC and was buried[110] in Poughkeepsie Rural Cemetery, Poughkeepsie, NY.

226.**Daniel R WEED** (Daniel R, Gardner, Samuel, Samuel, John, John, Jonas) was born[119] 1858 in New York.

Daniel married (1) **Mary UNKNOWN**. Mary was born[120] 1855 in New York.

They had the following children:

436 F i. **Theresa M WEED** was born[120] 1872 in New York.

437 F ii. **Emma L WEED** was born[120] 1873 in New York.

438 M iii. **Daniel R WEED** was born[59] Jun 1880 in New York.

439 F iv. **Florence L WEED** was born[59] Apr 1885 in New York.

Daniel also married[59] (2) **Annie E CARMICHAEL**. Annie was born[59] 1868 in New York.

They had the following children:

440 F v. **Ludella WEED** was born[59] Sep 1893 in New York.

+ 441 M vi. **Thurlow WEED** was born 27 Jun 1898 and died

---

[119]1860 Federal Census, Fishkill, Dutchess, NY.
[120]1880 Federal census, Fishkill, Dutchess, NY Dis 38.

Sep 1978.

442 F vii. **Edith WEED** was born[121] 1908 in New York.

227.**Juliette WEED** (Daniel Tompkins, David, Samuel, Samuel, John, John, Jonas) was born[122] 24 Mar 1843 in Middle Hope, Orange, NY. She died[122] 20 Mar 1906 in Newburgh, Orange, NY and was buried[122] in Cedar Hill Cemetery, Newburgh, NY.

Juliette married[122] **Leander CLARK JR** on 8 Feb 1865. Leander died[122] 19 Sep 1906 and was buried[122] in Cedar Hill Cemetery, Newburgh, NY.

They had the following children:

+ 443 F i. **Florence Bird CLARK** was born 1866 and died 3 Nov 1932.

444 M ii. **Edson L CLARK** was born[21] 1871.

445 M iii. **George A CLARK** was born[21] 1875.

446 F iv. **Bridget RYAN** was born 1871.

> BIOGRAPHY: Bridget was adopted.

228.**Jonathan Irving WEED** (Daniel Tompkins, David, Samuel, Samuel, John, John, Jonas) was born[122] 26 Feb 1846 in Newburgh, Orange, NY. He died[122] 4 Nov 1932 in Denver, CO and was buried[122] in Oswego, NY.

Jonathan married[8] **Susan Eliza LIPPENCOTT** on 26 Aug 1868 in Oswego, Oswego, NY. Susan was born[123] 29 Apr 1845 in New York, New York, NY. She died[123] 7 Feb 1905 in Brooklyn, Kings, NY.

They had the following children:

447 F i. **Alice T WEED** was born[124] 1869.

448 M ii. **Floyd WEED** was born[124] 1874.

---

[121]1910 Federal Census, Fishkill, Dutchess, NY Dis 48.
[122]Daniel Tompkins Weed Family Bible.
[123]NSDAR. "#320341 paper of Grace Weed Lippold."
[124]1880 Federal census, Oswego, NY.

Floyd Weed

449   F   iii.   **Jessie Louise WEED** was born[124] 1878.

+   450   M   iv.   **Frank I WEED** was born 15 May 1879 and died 16 Mar 1948.

+   451   F   v.   **Grace WEED** was born 25 Dec 1883.

231.**Adolphus WEED** (Daniel Tompkins, David, Samuel, Samuel, John, John, Jonas) was born[122] 3 Apr 1852 in Middle Hope, Orange, NY. He died[122] 25 Jul 1934 in Pine Bush, Orange, NY and was buried[122] in Woodlawn Cemetery, New Windsor, NY.

Adolphus married[122] (1) **Gertrude BELKNAP**, daughter of Sands BELKNAP and Catherine UNKNOWN, on 28 Apr 1874. Gertrude was born[125] Mar 1854. She died 30 Sep 1913 and was buried in Woodlawn Cemetery, New Windsor, NY.

They had the following children:

452   F   i.   **Florence G WEED** was born[125] May 1887. She died[122,126] 14 Dec 1906 and was buried in Woodlawn Cemetery, New Windsor, NY.

---

[125] 1900 Federal Census, Newburgh, NY 2nd Ward.
[126] Newburgh Daily Journal, Tuesday, December 18 1906.

Florence married **George B FREER**.

Adolphus had a relationship with (2) **Lillian LENT**.

They had the following children:

    453   F   ii. **Myrtle WEED** was born[127] 21 Nov 1909 in Newburgh, Orange, NY. She died[128] 22 Jul 1999 in Pine Bush, Orange, NY and was buried[128] in New Prospect Cemetery, Pine Bush, NY.

                    Myrtle married **Henry LUTZ**.

233.**Mary DUNN** (Abigail WEED, David, Samuel, Samuel, John, John, Jonas) was born[129] 25 Mar 1850 in Middle Hope, Orange, NY. She died[129] 18 Jun 1896 in Walden, Orange, NY.

Mary married[129] **Charles Butterworth FOWLER** on 9 Jan 1867 in Marlboro, Ulster, NY. Charles was born[129] 25 Mar 1847 in Middle Hope, Orange, NY. He died 19 Jul 1909 in Walden, Orange, NY.

They had the following children:

    454   F   i. **Cornelia D FOWLER** was born 23 Nov 1867. She died Apr 1952.

                    Cornelia married **John William PENNEY**. John was born 30 Jun 1861. He died Sep 1908.

+   455   F   ii. **Rebecca Grove FOWLER** was born 18 Apr 1869 and died 8 Oct 1944.

    456   M   iii. **William H FOWLER** was born 4 Aug 1870 in Middle Hope, Orange, NY. He died 2 Sep 1944.

    457   M   iv. **Charles Edward FOWLER** was born[130] Nov 1872 in New York.

    458   F   v. **Minerva May FOWLER** was born[131] 1875 in

---

[127]Social Security Application, Application of Myrtle Weed.
[128]Times Herald Record, Monday, July 26, 1999.
[129]Orange County, NY Genealogical Society, Notes of Gertrude Watkins Gray.
[130]1900 Federal Census, Montgomery, Orange, NY Dis 30.
[131]1880 Federal census, Montgomery, Orange, NY Dis

New York. She died Mar 1940.

Minerva married **Frederick CONKLIN**.

459 M vi. **David Laverne FOWLER** was born[131] 1876 in New York. He died 2 Jan 1939.

David married **Margaret BURTBACK**.

460 F vii. **Mary Eva FOWLER** was born 23 Dec 1879. She died 20 Oct 1963.

Mary married **Victor M TERWILLIGER**.

235. **Alphonso Weed DUNN** (Abigail WEED, David, Samuel, Samuel, John, John, Jonas) was born[129] 14 Mar 1854 in Middle Hope, Orange, NY. He died[129] 30 Aug 1930 in Walden, Orange, NY.

Alphonso married[129] **Ann Eliza ROOSA** on 26 Mar 1879 in Walden, Orange, NY. Ann was born[129] 19 Feb 1852. She died[129] 24 May 1925 in Walden, Orange, NY.

They had the following children:

461 F i. **Leah Roosa DUNN** was born[129] 15 Jun 1884 in Walden, Orange, NY. She died[129] 30 Dec 1962 in Walden, Orange, NY.

Leah married[129] **Thomas Millspaugh WATKINS** on 7 Jun 1905 in Walden, Orange, NY. Thomas was born[129] 6 Jun 1879. He died[129] 3 Dec 1957 in Walden, Orange, NY.

236. **David Lamorn DUNN** (Abigail WEED, David, Samuel, Samuel, John, John, Jonas) was born[129] 7 Aug 1856 in Johnstown, Barry, MI. He died[129] 1916 and was buried[129] in Mt. Auburn Cemetery, Hopkinton, MA.

David married[129] **Flora Abby DAVENPORT** on 19 Mar 1894 in Hopkinton, Middlesex, MA.

They had the following children:

462 M i. **Edward DUNN** was born[129] 13 Dec 1897.

238. **Emma Rebecca DUNN** (Abigail WEED, David, Samuel, Samuel, John, John, Jonas) was born[129] 1 Jul 1863 in Rondout, Ulster, NY. She was buried[129] in Wallkill Valley Cemetery, Walden, NY.

24.

Emma married[129] **Charles G SINSABAUGH** on 31 Oct 1884. Charles was born[129] 15 Jan 1860.

They had the following children:

    463   F   i. **Nettie SINSABAUGH** was born[129] 11 Apr 1889.

                    Nettie married **Grover CONKLIN**[129].

252. **Silas GARDNER** (Levi Weed GARDNER, Anna WEED, Samuel, Samuel, John, John, Jonas) was born[135] 1852 in New York.

Silas married **Catherine UNKNOWN**. Catherine was born[136] 1858 in New Jersey.

They had the following children:

    469   M   i. **William H GARDNER** was born[136] Apr 1874 in New Jersey.

+   470   M   ii. **George F GARDNER** was born Dec 1877.

+   471   M   iii. **Thomas B GARDNER** was born Apr 1881.

    472   F   iv. **Sadie GARDNER** was born[137] Jul 1884 in New Jersey.

+   473   M   v. **Silas Lester GARDNER** was born 14 Jan 1890.

+   474   F   vi. **Lydia GARDNER** was born Jul 1894.

253. **Alpharetta GARDNER** (Levi Weed GARDNER, Anna WEED, Samuel, Samuel, John, John, Jonas) was born[135,138] Jul 1854 in New York.

Alpharetta married **James YATES**. James was born[138,139] Oct 1851 in New Jersey.

They had the following children:

    475   F   i. **Maria YATES** was born[139] 1873 in New Jersey.

---

[135] 1860 Federal Census, Perth Amboy, Middlesex, NJ.
[136] 1880 Federal census, Perth Amboy, Middlesex, NJ Dis 120.
[137] 1900 Federal Census, Perth Amboy, Middlesex, NJ Ward 6 Dis 54.
[138] 1900 Federal Census, Perth Amboy, Middlesex, NJ Ward 4 Dis 52.
[139] 1880 Federal census, Perth Amboy, Middlesex, NJ Dis 128.

476 F ii. **Martha YATES** was born[139] 1875 in New Jersey.

477 F iii. **Edna YATES** was born[139] 1876 in New Jersey.

478 M iv. **Arthur YATES** was born[138,140] 25 Jul 1880 in New Jersey.

479 F v. **Maude YATES** was born[138] Jan 1884 in New Jersey.

+ 480 M vi. **Lorenzo YATES** was born 11 Jan 1886.

259.**Anthony S THOMAS** (Mahala GARDNER, Anna WEED, Samuel, Samuel, John, John, Jonas) was born[23] 1845 in New York.

Anthony married[141] **Emma RUSSELL**. Emma was born[141] 1850 in New York.

They had the following children:

481 F i. **Emma J THOMAS** was born[141] 1876 in New York.

264.**Abbey S WEAR** (Martha Weed GARDNER, Anna WEED, Samuel, Samuel, John, John, Jonas) was born[142,143] 16 Nov 1852 in New York. She died[144] 3 Oct 1881 in Topeka, Shawnee, KS and was buried[143] in Topeka Cemetery, Topeka, KS.

Abbey married[145] **Anson J CHESTER**.

They had the following children:

482 F i. **Daisy M CHESTER** was born[146] Sep 1875 in New York.

483 M ii. **Roy CHESTER** was born[145] 1877 in Kansas.

268.**Ina R WEAR** (Martha Weed GARDNER, Anna WEED, Samuel, Samuel, John, John, Jonas) was born[147,148] Aug 1862 in Pittston,

---

[140]World War One Registration.
[141]1880 Federal census, Brooklyn, Kings Co., NY Dist 94.
[142]1860 Federal Census, Pittston, Luzerne, PA.
[143]Records of the Topeka, KS cemetery.
[144]The Commonwealth, Tuesday, October 4, 1881.
[145]1880 Federal census, Topeka, Shawnee, KS Dis 6.
[146]1900 Federal Census, Buffalo, Erie, NY Ward 24 Dis 199.
[147]1880 Federal census, Marena, Hodgeman, KS.
[148]1900 Federal Census, Topeka, Shawnee, KS Ward 4

Luzerne, PA. She died between 1900-1904.

Ina married[149] **Byron F. KEEFER** on 2 Oct 1883 in Topeka, Shawnee, KS. Byron was born[148] Jun 1855 in Michigan.

They had the following children:

    484   M   i.   **Harold KEEFER** was born[148] Oct 1884 in Kansas.

    485   M   ii.   **Eugene G KEEFER** was born[143] 6 Nov 1886 in Topeka, Shawnee, KS. He died[143] 23 Nov 1891 in Topeka, Shawnee, KS and was buried[143] in Topeka Cemetery, Topeka, KS.

    486   M   iii.   **Sidney KEEFER** was born[148] Oct 1891 in Kansas.

269. **Theodore Graham WEAR** (Martha Weed GARDNER, Anna WEED, Samuel, Samuel, John, John, Jonas) was born[143,147] 22 Aug 1865 in Pittston, Luzerne, PA. He died[143] 22 May 1931 in Topeka, Shawnee, KS and was buried[143] in Topeka Cemetery, Topeka, KS.

Theodore married **Marie PRICE**. Marie was born[150] Oct 1875 in Kansas.

They had the following children:

    487   M   i.   **Millard Price WEAR** was born[93,150,151] 21 Aug 1896 in Pittsburg, Crawford, KS. He died[93] Jul 1970 in New York, New York, NY.

    488   M   ii.   **Theodore Graham WEAR JR** was born[93,152] 23 Sep 1902 in Joplin, Jasper, MO. He died[93] Jul 1974 in New York, New York, NY.

                  Theodore married[149] **Verna Anne MCCUE** on 23 Aug 1930 in Topeka, Shawnee, KS.

270. **Norman S WEAR** (Martha Weed GARDNER, Anna WEED, Samuel, Samuel, John, John, Jonas) was born[147] Mar 1868 in

---

Dis 162.
[149]Shawnee county, KS Marriage records.
[150]1900 Federal Census, Joplin, Jasper, MO Ward 3 Dis 37.
[151]Social Security Application, Application of Millard P. Wear.
[152]Social Security Application, Application of Theodore G. Wear.

Pittston, Luzerne, PA. He died[143,153] 21 Feb 1932 in Topeka, Shawnee, KS and was buried[143] in Topeka Cemetery, Topeka, KS.

Norman married[149] **Grace DIEUST** on 14 Oct 1891 in Topeka, Shawnee, KS. Grace was born[154] Jul 1870 in Ohio.

They had the following children:

    489   F   i.   **Marian WEAR** was born[154] Oct 1892 in Kansas.

273.**Ellen V BROWN** (Nathaniel M BROWN, Jane WEED, Samuel, Samuel, John, John, Jonas) was born[155,156,157] 19 Feb 1850 in Newburgh, Orange, NY. She died[157] 17 Dec 1909.

Ellen married[157] **James MAPES** on 21 Feb 1872. James was born[157,158] 1 Jun 1843 in New York. He died[157] 12 Feb 1926.

They had the following children:

    490   F   i.   **Katherine MAPES** was born[157,158] 4 Nov 1872 in New York. She died[157] 2 Feb 1925.

                       Katherine married[157,159] **Elmer F MARKEY** on 6 Mar 1907.

+   491   F   ii.   **Caroline MAPES** was born 4 Nov 1872 and died 3 Jan 1905.

285.**Silas BROWN** (Silas BROWN, Jane WEED, Samuel, Samuel, John, John, Jonas) was born[156] 11 Apr 1854 in Newburgh, Orange, NY. He died 19 Jan 1927 in Wappingers Falls, Dutchess, NY.

Silas married **Maria HAYES**. Maria was born 18 Feb 1855.

They had the following children:

    492   M   i.   **William BROWN** was born[160] 1874 in

---

[153]Topeka Journal, February 22, 1932.
[154]1900 Federal Census, Topeka, Shawnee, KS Ward 6 Dis 166.
[155]Portrait and Biographical record of Rockland and Orange Counties, Page 461.
[156]1860 Federal Census, Newburgh, Orange, NY.
[157]Mapes family association of New York, The Mapes family in America.
[158]1900 Federal Census, New Windsor, Orange, NY Dis 47.
[159]1910 Federal Census, Hamptonburgh, Orange, NY.
[160]1880 Federal census, Wappinger, Dutchess, NY Dis 72.

Wappingers Falls, Dutchess, NY.

+ 493 F ii. **Minnie BROWN** was born 2 Oct 1878 and died 20 Mar 1929.

494 M iii. **Bert BROWN** was born[161] Dec 1880 in Wappingers Falls, Dutchess, NY.

299.**Frances Amelia BOOZ** (Martha Jane WEED, Silas Gardner, Samuel, Samuel, John, John, Jonas) was born[162] 10 Jan 1846 in Brooklyn, Kings, NY. She died[163,164] 8 Feb 1893 in Brooklyn, Kings, NY and was buried[163] in Green-Wood Cemetery, Brooklyn, NY.

Frances married **Harman C SCHULTZ** on 7 May 1866 in Brooklyn, Kings, NY.

They had the following children:

495 M i. **William SCHULTZ** was born[165] 1868 in New York.

300.**Elizabeth L BOOZ** (Martha Jane WEED, Silas Gardner, Samuel, Samuel, John, John, Jonas) was born 8 Feb 1848 in Brooklyn, Kings, NY.

Elizabeth married **Luke R SALT** on 19 Mar 1865 in Brooklyn, Kings, NY.

They had the following children:

+ 496 M i. **Albert L SALT** was born Oct 1865.

+ 497 M ii. **Harman Schultz SALT** was born May 1870.

498 M iii. **Daniel Ireland SALT** was born[140,166] 4 Sep 1877 in Brooklyn, Kings, NY.

+ 499 F iv. **Frances M SALT** was born Nov 1880.

---

[161]1900 Federal Census, Wappingers Falls, Dutchess, NY Dis 44.
[162]1850 Federal Census, Brooklyn, Kings, NY Ward 11.
[163]Records of Green-Wood cemetery, Brooklyn, NY.
[164]Brooklyn Daily Eagle, Thursday November 9, 1893.
[165]1870 Federal Census, Brooklyn, Kings, NY Ward 10.
[166]1880 Federal census, Brooklyn, Kings, NY Dis 24.

301.**Winfield Scott BOOZ** (Martha Jane WEED, Silas Gardner, Samuel, Samuel, John, John, Jonas) was born[162] 1850 in New York. He died[167] 3 Nov 1893 in Brooklyn, Kings, NY.

Winfield married **Mary HARRINGTON** on Sep 1869. Mary died[168] 30 Aug 1894 in Brooklyn, Kings, NY and was buried[168] in Holy Cross Cemetery, Brooklyn, NY.

They had the following children:

+   500   F   i.   **Mary BOOZ** was born Feb 1871.

307.**Emily TURNBULL** (Frances M WEED, Silas Gardner, Samuel, Samuel, John, John, Jonas) was born[169] 1848 in New York.

Emily married[170] **John HEFLEBOWER**. John was born[170] 1848 in Virginia.

They had the following children:

   501   F   i.   **Eva HEFLEBOWER** was born[170] 1873 in Maryland.

   502   F   ii.   **Annina HEFLEBOWER** was born[170] 1875 in Maryland.

+   503   F   iii.   **Emily H HEFLEBOWER** was born 1879.

---

[167]Brooklyn Daily Eagle, Saturday, November 4, 1893.
[168]Brooklyn Daily Eagle, Saturday, October 2, 1894.
[169]1870 Federal Census, Baltimore, Baltimore, MD Ward 18.
[170]1880 Federal census, Baltimore, Baltimore, MD Dis 181.
[171] 1900 Federal census, Hamptonburgh, Orange, NY Dis 15.

Ninth Generation

310.**Mary HOLMES**[1] (Martha MERRITT, Mary WEED, Samuel, Nathaniel, Samuel, John, John, Jonas) was born[2] 4 Mar 1819.

Mary married **Cornelius WARING**[1].

They had the following children:

    504   F   i.   **Adelaide WARING**[2] was born[3] 1840 in New York.

                   Adelaide married **Aaron GARDNER**[2], son of Daniel D GARDNER and Catherine UNKNOWN. Aaron was born[4] 1839 in Orange County, NY.

    505   F   ii.   **Justine WARING**[2] was born[3] 1842 in New York.

                   Justine married **Woolsey FOWLER**[2].

    506   F   iii.   **Charlotte WARING**[2] was born[3] 1844 in New York.

                   Charlotte married **William CLARK**[2].

    507   F   iv.   **Emma WARING**[2] was born[5] 1847 in New York.

                   Emma married **Unknown POLHAMUS**[2].

    508   M   v.   **Cornelius WARING JR**[2] was born[3] 1850 in New York.

311.**Charlotte HOLMES**[6] (Martha MERRITT, Mary WEED, Samuel,

---

[1]Frank L. Crawford, Morris D' Camp Crawford and his wife, Charlotte Holmes Crawford: their lives, ancestries and descendants, Page 35.
[2]Frank L. Crawford, Morris D' Camp Crawford and his wife, Charlotte Holmes Crawford: their lives, ancestries and descendants, Page 49.
[3]1860 Federal Census, Newburgh, Orange, NY.
[4]1850 Federal Census, Newburgh, Orange, NY.
[5]1860 Federal Census, Newburgh, Orange, NY.
[6]Frank L. Crawford, Morris D' Camp Crawford and his wife, Charlotte Holmes Crawford: their lives, ancestries and descendants, Page 34.

Nathaniel, Samuel, John, John, Jonas) was born[7] 14 Apr 1822. She died[8] 6 Aug 1886 and was buried[8] in White Plains Rural Cemetery, White Plains, NY.

Charlotte married[7] **Morris D'Camp CRAWFORD**[1] on 29 Oct 1844.

They had the following children:

509 F   i.   **Charlotte Holmes CRAWFORD** was born[8] Mar 1846. She died[8] 1 Apr 1846.

510 F   ii.   **Caroline CRAWFORD** was born[8] 4 Oct 1847. She died[8] 19 Dec 1921.

        Caroline married[9] **John Edgar LEAYCRAFT**[8] on 25 Nov 1874. John died[8] 3 Jul 1916.

511 M   iii.   **Gilbert Holmes CRAWFORD** was born[8] 4 Oct 1849. He died[8] 13 Oct 1915.

        Gilbert married[8] (1) **Marion C FULLER**[8] on 2 Oct 1873. Marion died[8] Nov 1873.

        Gilbert also married[8] (2) **Sarah E MERRITT**[8] on 30 Dec 1879.

512 M   iv.   **Morris Barker CRAWFORD** was born[8] 26 Sep 1852.

        Morris married[8] **Caroline Laura RICE**[8] on 25 Dec 1883.

513 M   v.   **Hanford CRAWFORD** was born[8] 12 Feb 1854. He died[8] 24 Jan 1930.

        Hanford married[8] **Mary Gertrude SMITH**[8] on 11 Nov 1886. Mary died[8] 27 Sep 1930.

514 M   vi.   **Frank Lindsay CRAWFORD** was born[8] 14 Oct

---

[7]Frank L. Crawford, Morris D' Camp Crawford and his wife, Charlotte Holmes Crawford: their lives, ancestries and descendants, Page 64.
[8]Frank L. Crawford, Morris D' Camp Crawford and his wife, Charlotte Holmes Crawford: their lives, ancestries and descendants, Page 66.
[9]Frank L. Crawford, Morris D' Camp Crawford and his wife, Charlotte Holmes Crawford: their lives, ancestries and descendants, Page 108.

1856.

Frank married **Genevieve BUCKLAND**[8]. Genevieve died[8] 24 Feb 1929.

515 M vii. **William Herbert CRAWFORD** was born[8] 22 Mar 1860. He died[8] 16 Jun 1908.

William married[8] **Mina PAINE** on 8 Oct 1889.

312.**Martha HOLMES**[1] (Martha MERRITT, Mary WEED, Samuel, Nathaniel, Samuel, John, John, Jonas) died[2] 19 May 1865 and was buried[2] in Cedar Hill Cemetery, Newburgh, NY.

Martha married **Edward GILBERT**[1].

They had the following children:

516 F i. **Annie GILBERT**[2].

517 F ii. **Grace GILBERT**[2].

Grace married **Oliver BEARD**[2].

518 M iii. **Edward Holmes GILBERT**[2].

Edward married **Virginia Burd BOYE**[2].

313.**Caleb MERRITT** (Josiah MERRITT, Mary WEED, Samuel, Nathaniel, Samuel, John, John, Jonas) was born[10] 1817 in Marlboro, Ulster, NY.

Caleb married[11] **Elsie BOLTON**[11] on 14 Jul 1845 in Newburgh, Orange, NY.

They had the following children:

519 F i. **Frances MERRITT**[11].

520 M ii. **Charles MERRITT**[11].

320.**Samuel K WEED** (Samuel, Samuel Kniffin, Samuel, Nathaniel, Samuel, John, John, Jonas) was born[12,13] 16 Dec 1841 in New York. He died[13] 9 Jun 1925 and was buried[13] in Wallkill Valley Cemetery, Walden, NY.

---

[10]Portrait and Biographical record of Rockland and Orange Counties, Page 541.
[11]Portrait and Biographical record of Rockland and Orange Counties, Page 542.
[12]1850 Federal Census, New Windsor, Orange, NY.
[13]Wallkill Valley Cemetery, Walden, NY.

Samuel married[14] **Emma MCCARTNEY** on 12 Jan 1881 in Little
Britain, Orange, NY. Emma was born[13] 26 Jan 1856. She died[13] 20
Oct 1930 and was buried[13] in Wallkill Valley Cemetery, Walden,
NY.

They had the following children:

521　M　　i.　**John J WEED** was born[15] 16 Mar 1882. He
died[15] 5 May 1882 and was buried[15] in Patton
Cemetery, Newburgh, NY.

522　M　　ii.　**Clarence K WEED** was born[13] 26 Aug 1883. He
died[13,16] 4 Dec 1912 and was buried[13] in
Wallkill Valley Cemetery, Walden, NY.

523　F　　iii.　**Miriam H WEED** was born[13] 19 Jan 1890. She
died[13,16] 30 Mar 1919 and was buried[13] in
Wallkill Valley Cemetery, Walden, NY.

524　F　　iv.　**Marie C WEED** was born[13] 27 Jun 1893. She
died[13] 6 Jan 1973 and was buried[13] in Wallkill
Valley Cemetery, Walden, NY.

525　M　　v.　**Arthur Morrison WEED** was born[17,18,19] 7 Aug
1898 in Rock Tavern, Orange, NY. He
died[19,20] 13 Mar 1966 in Rock Tavern,
Orange, NY and was buried[19] in St. Mary's
Cemetery, Montgomery, NY.

Arthur married **Johanna F MURPHY**[19,21].
Johanna was born[21] 1889 in New York.

---

[14]Orange County, NY Genealogical Society,
Marriage Notices from the Goshen Independent
Republican.
[15]Orange County, NY Genealogical Society, Records
from Newburgh, New Windsor and other nearby
towns.
[16]The Historical Society of Newburgh Bay and the
Highlands, Account book and diary of Jane
Morrison Weed.
[17]1900 Federal Census, New Windsor, Orange, NY
Dis 47.
[18]World War One Registration.
[19]Times Herald Record, Tuesday, March 15, 1966.
[20]Social Security Death Index.
[21]1930 Federal Census, New Windsor, Orange, NY
Dis 83.

322. **Israel Beatty WEED** (Charles, Samuel Kniffin, Samuel, Nathaniel, Samuel, John, John, Jonas) was born[13] 19 Dec 1841. He died[13,16] 26 Mar 1899 and was buried[13] in Wallkill Valley Cemetery, Walden, NY.

Israel married **Mary Crist TICE,** daughter of Charles Winfield TICE and Charlotte UNKNOWN. Mary was born[13] 20 Aug 1841. She died[13,16] 4 May 1910 and was buried[13] in Wallkill Valley Cemetery, Walden, NY.

They had the following children:

    526   M   i.   **Raphael Ashton WEED** was born[13] 21 Jun 1873. He died[13] 16 Nov 1931 and was buried[13] in Wallkill Valley Cemetery, Walden, NY.

                                Raphael married **Gertrude May BUSHFIELD.** Gertrude was born[13] 29 Dec 1876. She died[13] 16 Mar 1927 and was buried[13] in Wallkill Valley Cemetery, Walden, NY.

324. **Sarah E WEED** (Charles, Samuel Kniffin, Samuel, Nathaniel, Samuel, John, John, Jonas) was born[22,23] Oct 1848 in New York.

Sarah married[16] **Isaac BODINE**[16] on 17 Jan 1882.

They had the following children:

    527   F   i.   **Edith Grace BODINE** was born[23] Dec 1876 in New York.

325. **Nathaniel King WEED**[24] (Nathaniel, Samuel Kniffin, Samuel, Nathaniel, Samuel, John, John, Jonas) was born[25] 1857 in New York. He died[16] 31 Dec 1899.

Nathaniel married[16] **Anna May CORWIN**[24], daughter of Isaac Little CORWIN and Margaret Jemima MARQUIS, on 25 Mar 1891. Anna died[16] 9 Jan 1899.

They had the following children:

    528   M   i.   **Clayton Bagshaw WEED** was born[24] 4 Apr 1893

---

[22] 1850 Federal Census, Montgomery, Orange, NY.
[23] 1900 Federal Census, Bronx, New York, NY Dis 1025.
[24] Social Security Application, Application of Clayton B. Weed.
[25] 1870 Federal Census, New Windsor, Orange, NY.

in Newburgh, Orange, NY. He died[26] 28 Dec
1964 in Los Angeles, Los Angeles, CA.

529 F   ii. **Natalie WEED** was born[156] Oct 1898 in
Newburgh, Orange, NY.

329.**Mary L WEED** (William Roe, Samuel Kniffin, Samuel, Nathaniel,
Samuel, John, John, Jonas) was born[27] 1851 in New York.

Mary married[14] **H.F. NICHOLS**[27] on 7 Jan 1874 in Little Britain,
Orange, NY.

They had the following children:

530 F   i. **Elmira NICHOLS**[27].

531 M   ii. **William R.W. NICHOLS**[27].

330.**Charles W WEED** (William Roe, Samuel Kniffin, Samuel,
Nathaniel, Samuel, John, John, Jonas) was born[27] 19 Jan 1853 in
Little Britain, Orange, NY.

Charles married[14] **Laura S KELSEY**[27] on 15 Sep 1875 in Brooklyn,
Kings, NY. Laura was born[28] Feb 1853 in New York. She died[16] 16
May 1921.

They had the following children:

532 M   i. **Irving Kelsey WEED**[27] was born[18] 17 Jun 1876.

                Irving married[16] **Sarah M ROBERSON**[16] on
27 Nov 1919.

533 F   ii. **Emma J WEED**[27] was born[28] May 1879 in New
York.

534 F   iii. **Orlena WEED**[27] was born[26,28] 7 May 1887 in
New York. She died[26] 10 Jun 1976 in Los
Angeles, Los Angeles, CA.

                Orlena married **Brewster S BEACH**[29]. The
marriage ended in divorce. Brewster was
born[29] 1889 in Connecticut.

---

[26]Ancestry.com, California Death Index 1940-1997.
[27]Portrait and Biographical record of Rockland
and Orange Counties, Page 163, 164.
[28]1900 Federal Census, Newburgh, Orange, NY Ward
4 Dis 40.
[29]1930 Federal Census, White Plains, Westchester,
NY Dis 355.

Brewster and Orlena were divorced[30] 29 Aug 1934 in Reno, NV.

They had the following children:

535 M iv. **Charles Freeman WEED**[27] was born[18,28] 11 Feb 1889 in Newburgh, Orange, NY.

536 M v. **Laurence WEED**[27] was born[28] Dec 1891 in New York.

537 M vi. **Harold Kelsey WEED**[27] was born[18,28] 19 Dec 1894 in Newburgh, Orange, NY.

331. **Elmira J WEED** (William Roe, Samuel Kniffin, Samuel, Nathaniel, Samuel, John, John, Jonas) was born[27] 1856 in New York.

Elmira married **J GARLOW**[27].

They had the following children:

538 M i. **Judson C GARLOW**[27].

539 M ii. **Charles G GARLOW**[27].

332. **Ashton Doane WEED** (William Roe, Samuel Kniffin, Samuel, Nathaniel, Samuel, John, John, Jonas) was born[31] Nov 1859 in New York.

Ashton married[16] **Ida Elizabeth HILTON** on 11 Mar 1885. Ida was born[31] Aug 1865 in New York.

They had the following children:

540 M i. **William Edgar WEED** was born[18,31] 18 Jan 1886 in New York.

  William married **Pauline UNKNOWN**[32]. Pauline was born[32] 1889 in New York.

541 F ii. **Florence M WEED** was born[31] Nov 1887 in New York.

542 F iii. **Grace WEED** was born[31] Jan 1891 in New York.

543 M iv. **Raymond Hilton WEED** was born[18,31] 19 Mar 1891 in Newburgh, Orange, NY.

---

[30]Nevada State Journal, Wednesday, August 29, 1934.
[31]1900 Federal Census, Newburgh, Orange, NY Ward 2 Dis 36.
[32]1920 Federal Census, Newburgh, Orange, NY Dis 141.

333. **Edgar V.K. WEED** (William Roe, Samuel Kniffin, Samuel, Nathaniel, Samuel, John, John, Jonas) was born 1861. He died[16,27] 16 Dec 1893 in Newburgh, Orange, NY.

Edgar married[16] **Martha D MILSOM**[27] on 26 Jan 1888.

They had the following children:

544   F   i.   **Martha D.F. WEED** "Mattie" was born[33] Aug 1887 in Tennessee.

545   F   ii.   **Ollie R WEED**[27] was born[33] Jan 1890 in Tennessee.

334. **Peter Cole STANTON** (Abby Jane MILBURN, Hester MARONEY, Elizabeth WEED, Samuel, Samuel, John, John, Jonas) was born[5] 4 Sep 1857. He died[34] 8 Mar 1913 and was buried[34] in Gardnertown Cemetery, Newburgh, NY.

Peter married[35] **Minnie K UNKNOWN**.

They had the following children:

546   F   i.   **Cora M STANTON** was born[35] Oct 1881.

547   F   ii.   **Jennie K STANTON** was born[35] Mar 1886.

         Jennie married[36] **Joseph H MCKAY**.

337. **Vaness T MILBURN** (Samuel J MILBURN, Hester MARONEY, Elizabeth WEED, Samuel, Samuel, John, John, Jonas) was born[37,38] Sep 1869.

Vaness married[38] **Augusta UNKNOWN**.

They had the following children:

548   M   i.   **Charles Harold MILBURN** was born[18,38] 26 Oct 1892 in Newburgh, Orange, NY.

         Charles married **Florence C UNKNOWN**.

---

[33]1900 Federal Census, Memphis, Shelby, TN Ward 4 Dis 68.
[34]Gardnertown Cemetery, Newburgh, NY.
[35]1900 Federal Census, Newburgh, Orange, NY Ward 5 Dis 41.
[36]1910 Federal Census, Newburgh, Orange, NY Ward 5 Dis 59.
[37]1880 Federal census, Newburgh, Orange, NY.
[38]1900 Federal Census, East Greenbush, Rensselaer, NY Dis 33.

Florence was born[39] 1892 in New York.

549 M   ii. **Fred MILBURN** was born[38] Jul 1895.

550 F   iii. **Dora MILBURN** was born[38] Dec 1898.

350.**Frank Walter HENNION** (Sarah Elizabeth MARONEY, Uriah MARONEY, Elizabeth WEED, Samuel, Samuel, John, John, Jonas) was born[18,40] 24 Feb 1885 in New York.

He had the following children:

551 M   i. **Robert B HENNION** was born[41] 1916 in New York.

353.**Charles Weed SCOTT** (Sarah Ann WEED, Charles, Samuel, Samuel, Samuel, John, John, Jonas) was born[42] Oct 1853.

Charles married[43] **Harriet B ELLIOTT**. Harriet was born[43] 1861 in New York.

They had the following children:

552 M   i. **Frank R SCOTT** was born[42] Mar 1889.

553 M   ii. **Howard E SCOTT** was born[42,44] Apr 1891 in New York.

554 F   iii. **Grace Mildred SCOTT** was born[42,44] Jul 1894 in New York.

                Grace married **Charles DURZIN**[44].

555 M   iv. **Kenneth A SCOTT** was born[42] Oct 1899 in New York. He died between 1900-1910.

355.**George Swalm SCOTT** (Sarah Ann WEED, Charles, Samuel, Samuel, Samuel, John, John, Jonas) was born[45] 12 Feb 1856 in

---

[39]1920 Federal Census, Rensselaer, Rensselaer, NY Ward 7 Dis 32.
[40]1900 Federal Census, Brooklyn, Kings, NY Ward 23 Dis 387.
[41]1920 Federal Census, Brooklyn, Kings, NY Dis 1070.
[42]1900 Federal Census, Brooklyn, Kings, NY Dis 384.
[43]Orange County, NY Genealogical Society, Notes of Elizabeth Horton.
[44]1920 Federal Census, Brooklyn, NY Dis 294.
[45]Middletown Times Herald, Saturday, March 19,

Middletown, Orange, NY. He died[45] 18 Mar 1932 in Middletown, Orange, NY and was buried[46] in Hillside Cemetery, Middletown, NY.

George married **Frances I MANN** "Fannie". Fannie died 13 Nov 1922 in Middletown, Orange, NY and was buried[46] in Hillside Cemetery, Middletown, NY.

They had the following children:

556   F   i.   **Nellie B SCOTT** was born Sep 1885. She died[47] 23 Jan 1915 in Newburgh, NY and was buried[48] in Hillside Cemetery, Middletown, NY.

Nellie married[49] **Smiley B RUMPH**. Smiley was born[50] 1884 in New York.

358. **William Sharp WEED** (John Hollister, Charles, Samuel, Samuel, Samuel, John, John, Jonas) was born[51] 25 Feb 1866 in Pleasant Valley, Sullivan, NY and was baptized[52] 26 Apr 1866 in Bloomingburg, NY. He died[51] 20 Nov 1954 in Tucson, AZ and was buried in Greenwood Cemetery, Brooklyn, NY.

William married[51] **Frances Maude CHAPIN**[51] on 27 Sep 1892.

They had the following children:

557   M   i.   **Franklin Chapin WEED** was born[20,51] 20 Apr 1895 in Brooklyn, Kings, NY. He died[20] 9 Nov 1981 in El Paso, TX.

Franklin married[51] **Alice Reba FAHS**[51] on 27 Sep 1922.

359. **Elliott WEED** (John Hollister, Charles, Samuel, Samuel, Samuel,

---

1932.
[46]Hillside Cemetery, Middletown, NY.
[47]Middletown Daily Times Press, Saturday, January 23, 1915.
[48]Hillside Cemetery, Middletown, NY burial records.
[49]Interview with Helen Cudney Groen, 4 Nov 2004.
[50]1910 Federal Census, Middletown, NY 3rd Ward Dis 30.
[51]Interview with Chapin B. Weed, 20 Sep 2004.
[52]Methodist Episcopal Church of Bloomingburg, NY records of Baptisms.

John, John, Jonas) was born 20 Jun 1868.

Elliott married[43] **Emma May WALKER.**

They had the following children:

558   M   i.   **George Irdman WEED** was born[51,53] 15 Jul 1899 in Middletown, Orange, NY. He died[51] 10 Jul 1989 in Nashua, NH.

George married **Ethel Clark CAMPBELL.** Ethel was born[51] 15 Nov 1900 in Brooklyn, Kings, NY. She died[51] 16 May 1976 in Hackettstown, NJ.

361.**J Spencer WEED** (John Hollister, Charles, Samuel, Samuel, Samuel, John, John, Jonas) was born 24 Dec 1879. He died[20] 11 Nov 1969 in Morristown, Morris, NJ.

J Spencer WEED married (1) **Hannah Broadley BOWMAN** on 14 Oct 1908.

They had the following children:

559   M   i.   **Douglas Bowman WEED** was born[54,55] 6 Aug 1909 in Brooklyn, Kings, NY. He died[20] Jul 1983.

Douglas married[56] **Dorothy GARRETT.**

560   F   ii.   **Janet Moran WEED** was born[54] 14 Nov 1912 in New Jersey.

Janet married[56] **Charles GOETZ.**

561   M   iii.   **J Spencer WEED JR.** was born[54] 20 May 1919 in Short Hills, New Jersey. He died[20] 28 Jul 1988 in Paradise Valley, Maricopa, AZ.

J Spencer WEED JR. married[57] **Helene DODGE**[57] on 25 Nov 1943 in Ft. Huachuca, AZ. Helene was born[57] 3 Sep 1920 in Douglas, Cochise, AZ. She died[57] 29 Oct 2004

---

[53] 1920 Federal Census, Bergen, Rutherford, NJ Dis 107.
[54] 1930 Federal Census, Summit, Union, New Jersey.
[55] Social Security Application, Application of Douglas B. Weed.
[56] Interview with Chapin B. Weed, 2 Oct 2004.
[57] Interview with Sally C. Weed, January 9, 2006.

in Tucson, Pima, AZ.

J Spencer WEED also married[43] (2) **Ethel Randall EDDY**.

366.**Guy L WEED** (John Floyd, Samuel B, Samuel, Samuel, Samuel, John, John, Jonas) was born[58,59,60] 17 Mar 1874 in Titusville, Crawford, PA. He died[61] 8 Aug 1907 in Rochester, Monroe, NY and was buried[61] in Mt. Hope Cemetery, Rochester, NY.

Guy married[59] **Charlotte G GROVER** on 1 Mar 1899 in Rochester, Monroe, NY.

They had the following children:

> 562 M   i. **Floyd WEED** was born[62] 23 Feb 1900 in Rochester, Monroe, NY. He died[61] 8 May 1909 in Rochester, Monroe, NY and was buried[61] in Mt. Hope Cemetery, Rochester, NY.

372.**Inez A WEED** (Ermon Romain, Samuel B, Samuel, Samuel, Samuel, John, John, Jonas) was born[63] 8 Dec 1875. She died 16 Mar 1920 and was buried[64] in Fairview Cemetery, Beacon, NY.

Inez married **Howard Coleman DUFF**. Howard was born 2 Aug 1876. He died 14 Oct 1957 and was buried[64] in Fairview Cemetery, Beacon, NY.

They had the following children:

> 563 F   i. **Mildred DUFF** was born[65] 20 Sep 1902. She died[20] Jan 1987 in Seaford, Nassau, NY.
>
>   Mildred married **Trevor Lloyd DAVIES**.

377.**Claude LUDINGTON** (Mary R WEED, Samuel B, Samuel,

58

[59]City of Rochester, NY Archives and records center. Historic Marriage records research site.
[60]Civil War pension file of John F. Weed.
[61]Office of Vital Records, County of Monroe, Rochester, NY.
[62]1900 Federal Census, Rochester, Monroe, NY Dist 120.
[63]1900 Federal Census, Matteawan, Dutchess, NY Dist 10.
[64]Fairview Cemetery, Beacon, NY.
[65]1910 Federal Census, Mt Vernon, Westchester, NY Dis 67.

Samuel, Samuel, John, John, Jonas) was born[18,62] 25 Dec 1875 in New York. He died[66] 2 Feb 1934 in Orlando, Orange, FL and was buried[67] 6 Feb 1934 in Mt. Hope Cemetery, Rochester, NY.

Claude married[68] **Susan M CAMPBELL**. Susan was buried[67] 2 Oct 1961 in Mt. Hope Cemetery, Rochester, NY.

They had the following children:

564 M   i.   **Charles LUDINGTON** was born[69] 1907. He was buried[67] 3 Jul 1962 in Mt. Hope Cemetery, Rochester, NY.

                    Charles married[70] **Hilda W UNKNOWN**.

565 F   ii.   **Mary L LUDINGTON** was born Aug 1908. She was buried[67] 21 Mar 1910 in Mt. Hope Cemetery, Rochester, NY.

566 F   iii.   **Ruth LUDINGTON** was born[68] 1915.

378.**Mabel C LUDINGTON** (Mary R WEED, Samuel B, Samuel, Samuel, Samuel, John, John, Jonas) was born[59] 1876 in Phillipsport, Sullivan, NY. She was buried[67] 8 May 1934 in Mt. Hope Cemetery, Rochester, NY.

Mabel married[59] **Walter W WYMAN** on 18 Jun 1895 in Rochester, Monroe, NY.

They had the following children:

567 F   i.   **Norma L WYMAN** was born[69] 1899 in New York.

                    Norma married[71] **Alfred T VANESS**. Alfred was born[71] 1896 in England.

568 M   ii.   **Marion E WYMAN** was buried[67] 14 Oct 1908 in

---

[66]Syracuse Herald, Saturday, February 3, 1934.
[67]Records of the Mt. Hope cemetery, Rochester, NY.
[68]1920 Federal Census, Pittsford, Monroe, NY Dis 42.
[69]1910 Federal Census, Rochester, Monroe, NY Ward 12 Dis 126.
[70]1930 Federal Census, Rochester, Monroe, NY Dis 179.
[71]1920 Federal Census, Rochester, Monroe, NY Ward 12 Dis 146.

Mt. Hope Cemetery, Rochester, NY.

381.**Sadie M REICK** (Delaphine WEED, Samuel B, Samuel, Samuel, Samuel, John, John, Jonas) was born[63] Dec 1883 in New York. She died Feb 1920 and was buried in Poughkeepsie Rural Cemetery, Poughkeepsie, NY.

Sadie married[43] **Robert Newton HESTON**.

They had the following children:

   569   M   i.   **Robert HESTON** was born[72] 1912 in New York.

   570   F   ii. **Delaphine HESTON** was born[72] 1914 in New York.

382.**Esther J REICK** (Delaphine WEED, Samuel B, Samuel, Samuel, Samuel, John, John, Jonas) was born[63] 30 Nov 1896 in Beacon, Dutchess, NY. She died[73] 20 Nov 1989 in Poughkeepsie, Dutchess, NY and was buried[74] in Poughkeepsie Rural Cemetery, Poughkeepsie, NY.

Esther married[43] **Harold W BAUER**. Harold died 1934.

They had the following children:

   571   F   i.   **Nancy BAUER** was born[74] 1926.

              Nancy married **James Michael HOOLIHAN**[75].

385.**Elsie Jane MARKS** (Mary Josephine EVENS, Jane WEED, Samuel, Samuel, Samuel, John, John, Jonas) was born Dec 1878 and was baptized[76] 3 Mar 1894 in New Prospect Church, Pine Bush, NY. She died[77,78] 13 Nov 1934 in Kingston, Ulster, NY and was buried[77] in Wiltwyck Cemetery, Kingston, NY.

Elsie married[77] **Richard D PETERS**.

---

[72]1910 Federal Census, Poughkeepsie, Dutchess, NY Ward 4 Dis 68.
[73]Poughkeepsie Journal, Tuesday, November 21, 1989.
[74]Interview with Nancy Bauer Hoolihan.
[75]Interview with Julie Crouse.
[76]New Prospect Church, Pine Bush, NY Church records.
[77]Interview with Geraldine Nathan, 9 Sep 2004.
[78]Kingston Daily Freeman, Wednesday, November 14, 1934.

They had the following children:

572　F　　i.　**Geraldine PETERS** was born[77] 1921.

Geraldine married[77] **Elmor NATHAN** on 1948 in Kingston, Ulster, NY.

391.**Mildred Marie CRUMB**[79] (Myrtie Delia WEED, John, Samuel, Samuel, Samuel, John, John, Jonas) was born[20] 11 Sep 1902. She died[20] Apr 1992 in Akron, Erie, NY and was buried[80] in Highland Cemetery, Cherry Creek, NY.

Mildred married[80] **Clare CUMMINGS** on 25 Oct 1927 in South Dayton, Chautauqua, NY. Clare was buried[81] in Highland Cemetery, Cherry Creek, NY.

They had the following children:

573　F　　i.　**Madolyn Mildred CUMMINGS**.

392.**Albertine F CRUMB**[79] (Myrtie Delia WEED, John, Samuel, Samuel, Samuel, John, John, Jonas) was born 1903. She died[80] in Versailles, Cattaraugus, NY.

Albertine married[80] **Clive HARVEY**. Clive was born 16 Nov 1896. He died Sep 1971.

They had the following children:

574　M　　i.　**Norman HARVEY**[80].

393.**Dale Gerald CRUMB**[79] (Myrtie Delia WEED, John, Samuel, Samuel, Samuel, John, John, Jonas) was born[82] 4 Apr 1908 in Cherry Creek, Chautauqua, NY. He died[20] Jan 1986 in Buffalo, Erie, NY.

Dale married[80] **Lena UNKNOWN**.

They had the following children:

575　M　　i.　**Melvin CRUMB**[80].

394.**Gladys Elsie CRUMB**[79] (Myrtie Delia WEED, John, Samuel,

---

[79]1910 Federal Census, Cherry Creek, Chautauqua, NY Dis 112.
[80]Interview with Madolyn Cummings, September 30, 2005.
[81]USgenweb.org, Cemetery records of Cherry Creek, NY.
[82]Social Security Application, Application of Dale G. Crumb.

Samuel, Samuel, John, John, Jonas) was born 6 Mar 1909. She died[81] 10 Dec 1934 and was buried[81] in Highland Cemetery, Cherry Creek, NY.

Gladys married[83] **Millard Nelson CHASE**. Millard was born 25 Oct 1905. He died[20] Nov 1986 in Fredonia, Chautauqua, NY and was buried[81] in Highland Cemetery, Cherry Creek, NY.

They had the following children:

| 576 | F | i. | **Lois Gladys CHASE** was born[80,83] 4 Aug 1926. |

>Lois married[80] **Cecil Blaine MAHLE**. Cecil was born 30 Nov 1923 in Moiola, Clarion, PA.

| 577 | M | ii. | **Millard Nelson CHASE JR**[80]. |

| 578 | F | iii. | **Ruth Jean CHASE**[80]. |

395. **Marjory Harriet WEED** (Herbert Odell, John, Samuel, Samuel, Samuel, John, John, Jonas) was born[83] 26 Oct 1915.

Marjory married[83] **Ernest Roswell HIGBEE** on 9 Jul 1936. Ernest was born[20] 8 Nov 1913. He died[20] 22 Jan 1996 in Eustis, FL.

They had the following children:

| 579 | F | i. | **Sylvia Ann HIGBEE** was born[84] 4 Jun 1942. |

>Sylvia married[83] (1) **Ronald E DAVIDSON** on 26 Jun 1965.

>Sylvia also married[83] (2) **Patrick L BAILEY** on 25 Aug 1991.

| 580 | M | ii. | **Keith Herbert HIGBEE** was born[84] 30 Mar 1945. |

>Keith married[83] **Linda SHERMAN** on 10 Feb 1968.

| 581 | F | iii. | **Maxine Carol HIGBEE** was born[84] 27 Dec 1947. |

>Maxine married[83] **John TUTTON** on 27 Aug 1965.

396. **William Lloyd Garrison WEED** (James Marshall, Levi, Samuel,

---

[83]Email from Sylvia Higbee Bailey.
[84]Email from Bob Weaver.

Samuel, Samuel, John, John, Jonas) was born[85] 17 Jul 1884 in
Walker Valley, Ulster, NY. He died[86] 25 Aug 1954 in Bronx, Bronx,
NY and was buried[87] in Walker Valley Cemetery, Walker Valley,
NY.

William and Adele Weed

William married **Adele SCHWETSCHER** on 24 Jun 1906. Adele
was born[88] 28 Oct 1880 in Germany. She died[88] 26 Oct 1971 in
Bronx, Bronx, NY and was buried[89] in Walker Valley Cemetery,
Walker Valley, NY.

They had the following children:

582　M　　i.　**Richard Marshall WEED** was born[92] 11 Dec
1908. He died[90] 4 Apr 1999.

---

[85]New York State Birth Certificate.
[86]New York, NY death certificate.
[87]Walker Valley, NY Cemetery.
[88]Interview with Richard Dippold.
[89]Walker Valley, NY cemetery records.

Richard Marshall Weed

Richard married **Mildred MATZ**. Mildred was born[90] 1 May 1911. She died[20] 2 Apr 1977 in Los Angeles, CA.

583 F ii. **Marie Adele WEED** was born[92] 13 Aug 1914. She died[88] 6 Apr 1992 and was buried[91] in Woodland Cemetery, Bronx, NY.

Marie married[88] **Frank DIPPOLD**.

397.**Lewis Horton WEED** "Cap" (James Marshall, Levi, Samuel, Samuel, Samuel, John, John, Jonas) was born[92] 4 Jul 1887 in Burlingham, Sullivan, NY. He died[93] 10 May 1968 in Walker Valley, Ulster, NY and was buried[87] in Walker Valley Cemetery, Walker Valley, NY.

---

[90]Interview with William M. Weed.
[91]Email from Gail Dippold Shoemaker.
[92]James Marshall Weed Family Bible.
[93]Interview with Birdy Weed Carroll.

Lewis Horton Weed

Cap married[76] **Alice Mabel RUSGROVE,** daughter of Charles RUSGROVE and Susannah BAGLEY, on 9 Oct 1906 in New Prospect Church Parsonage, Pine Bush, NY. Alice was born[93] 2 Jan 1888 in Birmingham, England. She died[94] 10 Jun 1964 in Newburgh, Orange, NY and was buried[87] in Walker Valley Cemetery, Walker Valley, NY.

They had the following children:

584 F i. **Lillian Belle WEED** was born[93] 5 Sep 1907 in Walker Valley, Ulster, NY. She died[95] 26 May 1984 in Liberty, Sullivan, NY and was buried[87] in Walker Valley Cemetery, Walker Valley, NY.

Lillian married[76] **John Floyd SMITH** "Floyd" on 4 Aug 1929 in Walker Valley, Ulster, NY.

585 M ii. **James Francis WEED** was born[92] 17 Sep 1909 in Walker Valley, Ulster, NY. He died[96] 5 May 1983 in Ellenville, Ulster, NY.

James married (1) **Irma L HULSE**, daughter

---

[94]Times Herald Record, Saturday, June 13 1964.
[95]Times Herald Record, Tuesday, May 29 1984.
[96]New York state death certificate.

of Harvey HULSE and Emma MILES, on 1 Aug 1931 in Amenia, Dutchess, NY. The marriage ended in divorce. Irma was born 23 Jul 1913 in Middletown, Orange, NY. She died[97] 28 Feb 1973 in Middletown, Orange, NY and was buried[98] in Wallkill Cemetery, Middletown, NY.

James also married (2) **Lillian B SINSABAUGH**, daughter of John R SINSABAUGH and Inez N SMITH, on 1 Nov 1942 in Pine Bush, Orange, NY. The marriage ended in divorce. Lillian was born[99] 1917.

James had a relationship with (3) **Astrid LILLEMOEN**.

James also married[100] (4) **Norma BRESCIANI** on 10 Apr 1965 in Pine Bush, NY. Norma was born[100] 16 Sep 1933 in Staten Island, NY.

586 F   iii.   **Claudia Mary WEED** "Dean" was born[93] 14 Sep 1911 in Walker Valley, Ulster, NY. She died[93] 3 Sep 1938 in Bristol, Hartford, CT and was buried in Bristol, CT.

Dean married[93] **Clarence RUSGROVE.**

587 M   iv.   **Lewis Horton WEED JR.** was born[92] 8 Dec 1913 in Walker Valley, Ulster, NY. He died[101] 15 Nov 1997 in Goshen, Orange, NY.

Lewis married[102] (1) **Eleanor ONUSKO** on 15 Jan 1943 in Walden, Orange, NY. The marriage ended in divorce. Eleanor was born[102] 30 Oct 1918 in Brooklyn, Kings, NY.

Lewis also married (2) **Rita Marie DALPE.**

---

[97]Times Herald Record, Friday, March 2 1973.
[98]Wallkill Cemetery, Middletown, NY.
[99]1930 Federal Census, Shawangunk, Ulster, NY Dis 59.
[100]Interview with Norma Bresciani Weed.
[101]Times Herald Record, Sunday, November 16 1997.
[102]Interview with Eleanor Onusko Gould.

Rita was born[103] 22 Apr 1945 in Flushing, Queens, NY. The marriage ended in divorce.

588 F   v.   **Alice Mabel WEED** was born[92] 16 Mar 1917 in Walker Valley, Ulster, NY. She died[104] 10 Apr 1980 in Albany, NY and was buried[87] in Walker Valley Cemetery, Walker Valley, NY.

Alice married **William Ryan WISEMAN**. William was born 25 Nov 1913. He died 19 May 1965 and was buried[87] in Walker Valley Cemetery, Walker Valley, NY.

589 M   vi. **Edward DaSilva WEED** was born[105] 31 Aug 1920 in Walker Valley, Ulster, NY.

Edward married (1) **Ruth SNIFFEN** on 31 Aug 1941 in Goshen, Orange, NY. Ruth was born[105] 12 May 1918. She died 11 Apr 1990 and was buried[87] in Walker Valley Cemetery, Walker Valley, NY.

Edward also married[106] (2) **Elaine TERWILLIGER** on 5 Sep 1992 in Wallkill, Ulster, NY. Elaine was born[106] 28 Apr 1925 in Newburgh, Orange, NY.

590 F   vii. **Evelyn Louise WEED** was born[107] 16 Nov 1922 in Walker Valley, Ulster, NY.

---

[103]Interview with Julie Dalpe Weed.
[104]Times Herald Record, Friday, April 11 1980.
[105]Interview with Merry Weed Johansen.
[106]Interview with Elaine Terwilliger Weed, 15 Nov 2004.
[107]Interview with Evelyn Weed Mitchell.

Evelyn Weed Mitchell

Evelyn married[107] **Everett Samuel MITCHELL** on 25 Jan 1945.

591 M viii. **Eugene Charles WEED** "Zeke" was born[108] 10 Jul 1925 in Walker Valley, Ulster, NY. He died[109] 14 Jan 2002 in Newburgh, Orange, NY and was buried[87] in Walker Valley Cemetery, Walker Valley, NY.

Zeke married[110] (1) **Priscilla Joan PHINNEY**, daughter of William Whyte PHINNEY and Elizabeth North KELLY, on 14 Feb 1943. The marriage ended in divorce. Priscilla was born[110] 8 Jun 1925 in Boston, Suffolk, MA. She died[110] 2 Mar 2006 in Montpelier, Washington, VT.

Zeke also married (2) **Priscilla GREENE**.

592 F ix. **Bernice Hortence WEED** "Birdy" was born[93] 2 Aug 1930 in Walker Valley, Ulster, NY.

Birdy married[93] **John CARROLL JR** on 26 Aug 1948 in Walker Valley, Ulster, NY. John

---

[108]Interview with Eugene C. Weed.
[109]Times Herald Record, Tuesday, January 15 2002.
[110]Times Herald Record, Tuesday, March 28, 2006.

114

was born[93] 8 Dec 1925 in Bridgeport, Fairfield, CT. He died[93] 29 Dec 1990 in Walker Valley, Ulster, NY and was buried[87] in Walker Valley Cemetery, Walker Valley, NY.

398. **Reubin Watson WEED** (James Marshall, Levi, Samuel, Samuel, Samuel, John, John, Jonas) was born[92] 8 Jul 1890 in Burlingham, Sullivan, NY. He died 24 Nov 1957 in Ulsterville, Ulster, NY and was buried[87] in Walker Valley Cemetery, Walker Valley, NY.

Reubin married[92] **Ethel May BOYCE** on 18 Jul 1913. Ethel was born[111] 1890. She died[111] 1952 and was buried[111] in New Prospect Cemetery, Pine Bush, NY.

They had the following children:

593   F   i.   **Thelma WEED** was born 21 Feb 1915. She died 14 Jul 1988 and was buried[111] in New Prospect Cemetery, Pine Bush, NY.

                    Thelma married **Francis T WARD**. Francis was born 23 Dec 1915. He died 19 Jan 1980 and was buried[111] in New Prospect Cemetery, Pine Bush, NY.

594   F   ii.   **Hazel WEED** was born[112] 24 Apr 1918.

                    Hazel married[112] **Melvin LYBOLT** on Sep 1936 in Pine Bush, NY. Melvin was born 12 Jul 1908. He died 25 Dec 1968 and was buried[111] in New Prospect Cemetery, Pine Bush, NY.

399. **Mabel Elsie WEED** (James Marshall, Levi, Samuel, Samuel, Samuel, John, John, Jonas) was born[92] 10 Feb 1898. She died[20] 26 Dec 1962 in San Francisco, CA.

Mabel married[92] (1) **Leslie David MAINES** on 23 Mar 1916.

They had the following children:

595   F   i.   **Dorothy Alma MAINES** was born[92] 11 Apr 1917.

596   F   ii.   **Mary Isabella MAINES** was born[92,113] 9 Jul

---

[111]New Prospect Cemetery, Pine Bush, NY.
[112]Interview with Hazel Weed Lybolt.
[113]Social Security Application, Application of

1921 in Middletown, Orange, NY. She died[20]
29 Jul 1994 in Massapequa Park, Nassau, NY.

Mary married[20] **Unknown SCHAEFER**.

Mabel also married (2) **Unknown FLETCHER**.

402.**Harry Marvon WEED** (George E, Levi, Samuel, Samuel, Samuel, John, John, Jonas) was born[18,114] 26 Dec 1894 in Walker Valley, Ulster, NY. He died[115] 14 Nov 1976 in Detroit, Wayne, MI.

Harry married[115] **Jennie M THOMPKINS**. Jennie was born Feb 1897 in New York.

They had the following children:

597　F　　i.　**Mildred WEED** was born[115] 1915 in New York.

598　M　　ii.　**Harry Marvon WEED JR.** was born[115] 27 Nov 1916 in New York. He died[115] 12 Oct 2003 in Carmichael, Sacrament, CA.

　　　　　　　Harry married[115] (1) **Patricia Marie JONES** on 4 Dec 1943 in Alameda, CA. The marriage ended in divorce. Patricia was born 28 Jun 1924 in Victor, Teller, Colorado. She died 15 Jan 2002 in Pittsburg, Alameda, CA.

　　　　　　　Harry also married[115] (2) **Helen SCOTT**. Helen died[20] 25 Jun 1987.

404.**Mary GIBBS** (Ida Jane WEED, Levi, Samuel, Samuel, Samuel, John, John, Jonas) was born[116] 29 Aug 1887. She died[116] 19 Sep 1941.

Mary married[116] **William HOLBERT** on 25 Dec 1907.

They had the following children:

599　M　　i.　**Darwin HOLBERT** was born[116] 15 Nov 1908. He died[116] 27 Dec 1986.

600　F　　ii.　**Dorothy HOLBERT**[116].

　　　　　　　Dorothy married[116] **Arthur SELONICK**.

Mary I. Maines.
[114]Social Security Application, Application of Harry M. Weed.
[115]Email from Kathleen Regina.
[116]Interview with Anna Jean Allen Hilliker.

601 M iii. **Earl HOLBERT** was born[116] 27 Jan 1916. He died[116] 11 Nov 1985.

602 M iv. **Ivan HOLBERT**[116].

603 M v. **Allen HOLBERT**[116].

604 F vi. **Marjorie HOLBERT**[116].

605 F vii. **Florence HOLBERT**[116].

606 M viii. **Lee HOLBERT**[116].

406.**Anna V GIBBS** (Ida Jane WEED, Levi, Samuel, Samuel, Samuel, John, John, Jonas) was born[116] 19 Jun 1895. She died[116] 24 Jun 1987.

Anna married[116] **Orren Frank ALLEN** on 22 Dec 1920. Orren died[116] 13 Apr 1964.

They had the following children:

607 M i. **Orren Glenn ALLEN** was born[116] 27 Mar 1923. He died[116] 2 May 1984.

Orren married[116] **Alice M CANFIELD** on 15 Sep 1946.

608 F ii. **Anna Jean ALLEN** was born[116] 8 Oct 1928.

Anna married[116] (1) **Clarence JUDKINS JR** on 29 Jun 1947. The marriage ended in divorce.

Anna also married[116] (2) **Frederick HILLIKER** on 3 Aug 1958.

609 M iii. **Gail Gibbs ALLEN** was born[116] 28 Jan 1932.

Gail married[116] **Florence Ann SEELEY** on 25 Nov 1951.

409.**Alice B GIBBS** (Ida Jane WEED, Levi, Samuel, Samuel, Samuel, John, John, Jonas) was born[116] 5 Nov 1905. She died[116] Nov 1964.

Alice married[116] **Chester LINDSAY** on 4 Dec 1923.

They had the following children:

610 F i. **Eleanor LINDSAY** was born[116] 24 Apr 1927.

Eleanor married[116] **Harry PRYSTOWSKI** on 1 Jul 1949. Harry was born 6 Sep 1925. He died 30 Jan 2004.

611 F ii. **Ruth LINDSAY** was born[116] 25 Aug 1931.

117

Ruth married **Otto KANOSPE** on 7 Mar 1951. Otto was born[116] 11 Jul 1909. He died[116] 3 Dec 1990.

415.**Warren Silas ROBERTS**[117] (Benjamin ROBERTS, Lavinia WEED, Gardner, Samuel, Samuel, John, John, Jonas) was born[18,117] 28 Jan 1888 in New York, New York, NY.

Warren married[117] **Christina GOLDMANN**. Christina was born 12 May 1897. She died 3 Sep 1985.

They had the following children:

612　F　　i.　**Henrietta Carolina ROBERTS** was born[118] 1916 in New York.

613　F　　ii.　**Claire Constance ROBERTS** was born[117] 21 Sep 1920 in New York, New York, NY.

416.**William Henry ROBERTS**[117] (Benjamin ROBERTS, Lavinia WEED, Gardner, Samuel, Samuel, John, John, Jonas) was born[117,119] 1892 in New York, New York, NY.

William married **Louise Christina SCHICKLER**[117].

They had the following children:

614　F　　i.　**Beatrice ROBERTS**[117] was born[117,119] 1916 in New York, New York, NY.

615　M　　ii.　**William Henry ROBERTS JR**[117] was born[117,119] 1920 in New York, New York, NY.

616　F　　iii.　**Virginia ROBERTS**[117] was born[117,120] 1927 in New York.

617　F　　iv.　**Lorraine ROBERTS**[117] was born[117,120] 1929 in New York.

618　M　　v.　**William Henry ROBERTS JR**[117].

421.**Milton N ROBERTS** (John J ROBERTS, Lavinia WEED, Gardner,

---

[117]Email from Kurt Sobina.
[118]1930 Federal Census, Manhattan, New York, NY Dis 1153.
[119]1920 Federal Census, Manhattan Assembly Dis 16, New York, NY Dis 1139.
[120]1930 Federal Census, Huntington, Suffolk, NY Dis 70.

Samuel, Samuel, John, John, Jonas) was born 1889. He died[121] 12 Mar 1979 in Cortlandt, Westchester, NY and was buried[121] in Poughkeepsie Rural Cemetery, Poughkeepsie, NY.

He had the following children:

> 619 F i. **Gertrude ROBERTS** was born[121] 20 Apr 1913. She died[121] 13 Oct 1976 in New York, New York, NY and was buried[121] in Poughkeepsie Rural Cemetery, Poughkeepsie, NY.

441.**Thurlow WEED** (Daniel R, Daniel R, Gardner, Samuel, Samuel, John, John, Jonas) was born[20,63] 27 Jun 1898 in New York. He died[20] Sep 1978 in Beacon, Dutchess, NY.

Thurlow married[122] **Helen UNKNOWN**.

They had the following children:

> 620 M i. **Donald WEED** was born[122] 1926 in New York.
>
> 621 M ii. **Thurlow N WEED** was born[122] 1927 in New York.

443.**Florence Bird CLARK** (Juliette WEED, Daniel Tompkins, David, Samuel, Samuel, John, John, Jonas) was born[37] 1866 in Newburgh, Orange, NY. She died 3 Nov 1932 in Brooklyn, Kings, NY and was buried in Cedar Hill Cemetery, Newburgh, NY.

Florence married **Charles H POST**.

They had the following children:

> 622 M i. **Everts Clark POST**.

450.**Frank Irving WEED** (Jonathan Irving, Daniel Tompkins, David, Samuel, Samuel, John, John, Jonas) was born[123] 15 May 1879 in Oswego, Oswego, NY. He died[123] 16 Mar 1948 in Decatur, GA.

---

[121]Records of Poughkeepsie Rural Cemetery, Poughkeepsie, NY.
[122]1930 Federal Census, Beacon, Dutchess, NY Dis 10.
[123]NSDAR, #390905 paper of Alice Weed Johnson.

Frank Irving Weed

Frank married[123] **Lucile GOODWIN** on 22 Apr 1908. Lucile was born[123] 9 May 1884 in New York, New York, NY.

They had the following children:

623 F   i.   **Margaret L WEED** was born[124] 1909.

624 F   ii. **Alice F WEED** was born[123] 17 May 1911 in New York, New York, NY.

Alice married[123] **Dr. Charles B JOHNSON** on 25 Dec 1930 in Atlanta, GA. Dr. was born[123] 29 Aug 1905.

Married by Rev. R.H.N. Moor

625 M   iii. **Arthur G WEED** was born[124] 1913.

626 F   iv. **Edith R WEED** was born[124] 1921.

451.**Grace WEED** (Jonathan Irving, Daniel Tompkins, David, Samuel, Samuel, John, John, Jonas) was born[125] 25 Dec 1883 in Oswego, Oswego, NY.

---

[124]1930 Federal Census, DeKalb County, GA Militia Dis 531.
[125]NSDAR, #350470 paper of Grace Lippold Freeman.

Grace married[125] **Frederick A LIPPOLD JR** on 6 Nov 1907. Frederick was born[125] 17 Sep 1884 in New York, New York, NY. He died[125] 10 Mar 1931 in Brooklyn, Kings, NY.

They had the following children:

627 F   i. **Grace LIPPOLD** was born[125] 6 Aug 1908 in Brooklyn, Kings, NY.

Grace married[125] **Charles Alden FREEMAN JR** on 31 Mar 1932 in Brooklyn, NY. Charles was born 7 Apr 1909.

Married by Rev. C.W. Roeder

455.**Rebecca Grove FOWLER** (Mary DUNN, Abigail WEED, David, Samuel, Samuel, John, John, Jonas) was born 18 Apr 1869. She died 8 Oct 1944.

Rebecca married **Charles Walter PENNEY**. Charles was born 26 Oct 1858. He died 30 Sep 1920.

They had the following children:

628 M   i. **David Benjamin PENNEY** was born 8 Apr 1889. He died Jan 1890.

629 M   ii. **Charles Edward PENNEY** was born 23 Jul 1890. He died 15 Mar 1980 in Goshen, Orange, NY.

Charles married **Lucinda Rebecca VAN LEUVAN**. Lucinda was born 4 Sep 1899. She died Dec 1972 in Walden, Orange, NY.

630 F   iii. **Fanny May PENNEY** was born 20 Jul 1892. She died Apr 1916 in Poughkeepsie, Dutchess, NY.

631 M   iv. **Decatur Butterworth PENNEY** was born 27 Mar 1896 in Walden, Orange, NY. He died 26 Jan 1987 in Newburgh, Orange, NY.

Decatur married **Adelaide PALEN**. Adelaide was born 4 Apr 1905. She died 2 May 1940 in Walden, Orange, NY.

632 F   v. **Mary Cornelia PENNEY** was born 15 Oct 1900.

633 M   vi. **Jonathan Weed PENNEY** was born 1 Mar 1905. He died 16 Jun 1968.

Jonathan married **Gladys M MCINTOSH**. Gladys was born 5 Jul 1906. She died 3 Apr 1995 in Fishkill, Dutchess, NY.

> 634 M vii. **Vernon Walter PENNEY** was born 23 May 1909. He died 9 Jul 1966.
>
> Vernon married **Martha HALEY**.

470. **George F GARDNER** (Silas GARDNER, Levi Weed GARDNER, Anna WEED, Samuel, Samuel, John, John, Jonas) was born[126] Dec 1877 in New Jersey.

George married[127] **Nellie UNKNOWN**. Nellie was born[127] 1882 in New Jersey.

They had the following children:

> 635 F i. **Cecelia GARDNER** was born[127] 1904 in New Jersey.
>
> 636 F ii. **Ella M GARDNER** was born[127] 1906 in New Jersey.
>
> 637 F iii. **Katherine Lydia GARDNER** was born[127] 1908 in New Jersey.
>
> 638 M iv. **William GARDNER** was born[128] 1911 in New Jersey.
>
> 639 M v. **George GARDNER** was born[128] 1914 in New Jersey.

471. **Thomas B GARDNER** (Silas GARDNER, Levi Weed GARDNER, Anna WEED, Samuel, Samuel, John, John, Jonas) was born[129] Apr 1881 in New Jersey.

Thomas married[127] **Mary CANARY**. Mary was born[127] 1882 in Connecticut. She died between 1920-1930.

They had the following children:

---

[126]1880 Federal census, Perth Amboy, Middlesex, NJ Dis 120.
[127]1910 Federal Census, Perth Amboy, Middlesex, NJ Ward 3 Dis 30.
[128]1920 Federal Census, Perth Amboy, Middlesex, NJ Ward 5 Dis 47.
[129]1900 Federal Census, Perth Amboy, Middlesex, NJ Ward 6 Dis 54.

640 F   i.   **Margaret GARDNER** was born[127] 1909 in New Jersey.

641 M   ii.   **Kenneth GARDNER** was born[130] 1912 in New Jersey.

642 M   iii.   **Rodger GARDNER** was born[131] 1924 in New Jersey.

473.**Silas Lester GARDNER** (Silas GARDNER, Levi Weed GARDNER, Anna WEED, Samuel, Samuel, John, John, Jonas) was born[18,129] 14 Jan 1890 in Perth Amboy, Middlesex, NJ.

Silas married[132] **Anna UNKNOWN**. Anna was born[132] 1889 in Poland.

They had the following children:

643 F   i.   **Charlotte GARDNER** was born[132] 1914 in Perth Amboy, Middlesex, NJ.

644 M   ii.   **Gerard GARDNER** was born[132] 1917 in Perth Amboy, Middlesex, NJ.

474.**Lydia GARDNER** (Silas GARDNER, Levi Weed GARDNER, Anna WEED, Samuel, Samuel, John, John, Jonas) was born[129] Jul 1894 in New Jersey.

Lydia married[133] **John FOSTER**. John was born[134] 1893 in New Jersey.

They had the following children:

645 F   i.   **Lydia FOSTER** was born[135] 1921 in New Jersey.

646 F   ii.   **Vera FOSTER** was born[135] 1923 in New Jersey.

647 F   iii.   **Mildred FOSTER** was born[135] 1929 in New

---

[130]1920 Federal Census, Perth Amboy, Middlesex, NJ Ward 3 Dis 40.
[131]1930 Federal Census, Perth Amboy, Middlesex, NJ Dis 74.
[132]1920 Federal Census, Perth Amboy, Middlesex, NJ Ward 3 Dis 39.
[133]1920 Federal Census, Perth Amboy, Middlesex, NJ Ward 1 Dis 35.
[134]1920 Federal Census, Perth Amboy, Middlesex, NJ Ward 1 Dis 35.
[135]1930 Federal Census, Perth Amboy, Middlesex, NJ Dis 64.

Jersey.

480. **Lorenzo YATES** (Alpharetta GARDNER, Levi Weed GARDNER, Anna WEED, Samuel, Samuel, John, John, Jonas) was born[18,136] 11 Jan 1886 in New Jersey.

Lorenzo married[137] **Jennie UNKNOWN**. Jennie was born[137] 1890 in New York.

They had the following children:

    648   F   i.   **Susan YATES** was born[137] 1914 in New York.

    649   M   ii.   **Harold YATES** was born[137] 1915 in New York.

    650   M   iii.   **Lawrence YATES** was born[137] 1916 in New York.

491. **Caroline MAPES** (Ellen V BROWN, Nathaniel M BROWN, Jane WEED, Samuel, Samuel, John, John, Jonas) was born[138] 4 Nov 1872. She died[138] 3 Jan 1905 and was buried[139] in Fostertown Cemetery, Newburgh, NY.

Caroline married[138] **Fred B WARING** on 21 Dec 1892. Fred was born[138] 18 Aug 1867. He died[138] 5 Dec 1908 and was buried[139] in Fostertown Cemetery, Newburgh, NY.

They had the following children:

    651   M   i.   **James Elmer WARING** was born[138] 16 Nov 1895.

493. **Minnie BROWN** (Silas BROWN, Silas BROWN, Jane WEED, Samuel, Samuel, John, John, Jonas) was born[140] 2 Oct 1878 in Wappingers Falls, Dutchess, NY. She died[140] 20 Mar 1929 in Watertown, Litchfield, CT.

Minnie married **Howard Cassius RANSOM** on 10 Jun 1903 in Wappingers Falls, Dutchess, NY. Howard was born 20 Jun 1882 in Poughkeepsie, Dutchess, NY.

They had the following children:

---

[136] 1900 Federal Census, Perth Amboy, Middlesex, NJ Ward 4 Dis 52.
[137] 1920 Federal Census, Manhattan, New York, NY Dis 421.
[138] Mapes family association of New York, The Mapes family in America.
[139] Fostertown cemetery, Newburgh, NY.
[140] Ancestry.com, Page Family Tree, 5 Nov 2005.

652 M   i.   **Leroy Howard RANSOM** was born 6 Dec 1907 in Poughkeepsie, Dutchess, NY.

496.**Albert L SALT** (Elizabeth L BOOZ, Martha Jane WEED, Silas Gardner, Samuel, Samuel, John, John, Jonas) was born[141,142] Oct 1865 in Brooklyn, Kings, NY.

Albert married[142] **Mary BERGEN**. Mary was born[142] Aug 1869 in New York.

They had the following children:

653 M   i.   **Lloyd Bergen SALT** was born[18,142] 18 Mar 1893 in Brooklyn, Kings, NY. He died[20] Aug 1964 in Massachusetts.

Lloyd married[143] **Katherine W UNKNOWN**. Katherine was born[143] 1894 in Massachusetts.

497.**Harman Schultz SALT** (Elizabeth L BOOZ, Martha Jane WEED, Silas Gardner, Samuel, Samuel, John, John, Jonas) was born[141,144] May 1870 in Brooklyn, Kings, NY.

Harman married **Clara Frances LITTLE** on 5 Sep 1894 in Pembroke, Merrimack, NH. Clara was born[144] Apr 1873 in New Hampshire.

They had the following children:

654 F   i.   **Lucy Little SALT** was born[144] Jul 1898 in New York.

499.**Frances M SALT** (Elizabeth L BOOZ, Martha Jane WEED, Silas Gardner, Samuel, Samuel, John, John, Jonas) was born[145] Nov 1880 in Brooklyn, Kings, NY.

Frances married[146] **Gilbert Vaughn OLDHAM** on 9 Apr 1902 in Brooklyn, Kings, NY. Gilbert was born[18] 20 Oct 1878.

---

[141]1880 Federal census, Brooklyn, Kings, NY Dis 24.
[142]1900 Federal Census, Brooklyn, Kings, NY Ward 24 Dis 429.
[143]1930 Federal Census, Newton, Middlesex, MA Dis 391.
[144]1900 Federal Census, Brooklyn, Kings, NY Ward 29 Dis 539.
[145]1900 Federal Census, Brooklyn, Kings, NY Ward 3 Dis 23.
[146]Brooklyn Daily Eagle, Sunday, April 13, 1902.

They had the following children:

655 M i. **Gordon V OLDHAM** was born[147] 1905 in Brooklyn, Kings, NY.

500.**Mary BOOZ** (Winfield Scott BOOZ, Martha Jane WEED, Silas Gardner, Samuel, Samuel, John, John, Jonas) was born[148] Feb 1871 in New York.

Mary married **John J BOLLINGER**. John was born[148] Jan 1865 in New York.

They had the following children:

656 M i. **Frank Xavier BOLLINGER** was born[18,148] 25 Aug 1892 in Brooklyn, Kings, NY.

Frank married **Beatrice HAGGERTY**. Beatrice was born[149] 1901 in New York.

657 M ii. **John BOLLINGER JR** was born[148] Jul 1896 in New York.

John married **Marie UNKNOWN**. Marie was born[150] 1901 in New York.

658 F iii. **Marian BOLLINGER** was born[151] 1900 in New York.

659 M iv. **Winfield Scott BOLLINGER** was born[151,152] 2 Sep 1902 in Brooklyn, Kings, NY. He died[20] Nov 1967 in Brooklyn, Kings, NY.

Winfield married **Helen UNKNOWN**. Helen was born[153] 1904 in Pennsylvania.

---

[147]1910 Federal Census, Brooklyn, Kings, NY Ward 24 Dis 670.
[148]1900 Federal Census, Brooklyn, Kings, NY Ward 32 Dis 573.
[149]1920 Federal Census, Brooklyn, Kings, NY Dis 217.
[150]1930 Federal Census, Brooklyn, Kings, NY Dis 1845.
[151]1910 Federal Census, Brooklyn, Kings, NY Ward 29 Dis 1015.
[152]New York City Births 1891-1902.
[153]1930 Federal Census, Brooklyn, Kings, NY Dis 1848.

503. **Emily H HEFLEBOWER** (Emily TURNBULL, Frances M WEED, Silas Gardner, Samuel, Samuel, John, John, Jonas) was born[154] 1879 in Maryland.

Emily married **Norman A HILL**. Norman was born[155] 1882 in Maryland.

They had the following children:

   660 M   i. **T. Gardner HILL** was born[20,155] 31 Jul 1912 in Canada. He died[20] Jan 1983 in Atlanta, Fulton, GA.

   661 M   ii. **N. Allen HILL** was born[155] 1916 in Maryland.

[154]1880 Federal census, Baltimore, Baltimore, MD Dis 181.
[155]1930 Federal Census, Baltimore, Baltimore, MD Dis 192.
[156]1900 Federal census, Newburgh, Orange, NY Ward 6 Dis 43

Index

BOYER
    Catherine Lucretia (207S -
        b.1862), 79
BRESCIANI
    Norma (397S - b.1933), 112
BROWN
    Addison W (92 - b.1817), 28
    Adelaide (274 - b.1852), 54
    Adelia (271 - b.1844), 54
    Albert (272 - b.1847), 54
    Alfred (286 - b.1857), 55
    Amy J (280 - b.1869), 55
    Ann Eliza (75S - b.1840), 45
    Anna (278 - b.1860), 55
    Anna Eliza (95 - b.1830), 28, 56
    Bert (494 - b.1880), 91
    Caroline (279 - b.1863), 55
    Charles (96 - b.1833), 28
    Charles D (346 - b.1888), 64
    Delia (289 - b.1870), 56
    Edward (288 - b.1861), 56
    Elenora (342 - b.1878), 64
    Ellen V (273 - b.1850), 54, 90
    Halsey W (143S - b.1850), 63
    Harriet (97 - b.1835), 28, 56
    Henrietta (277 - b.1859), 55
    Henry H (343 - b.1879), 64
    Hosea (57S - b.1795), 28
    Jessie (275 - b.1854), 55
    Laura (287 - b.1860), 56
    Lavinia (283 - b.1845), 55
    Mary (282 - b.1843), 55
    Matilda (98 - b.1840), 28
    Mattie V (345 - b.1886), 64
    Mervin (284 - b.1849), 55
    Minnie (493 - b.1878), 91, 124
    Nathaniel M (93 - b.1819), 28,
        54
    Sally May (344 - b.1881), 64
    Silas (285 - b.1854), 55, 90
    Silas (94 - b.1821), 28, 55
    Spencer G (276 - b.1857), 55
    Tressa (281), 55
    William (492 - b.1874), 90
BUCKLAND
    Genevieve (311S - d.1929), 95
BULLARD
    Nathan (- b.1754), 24
    Olive (48S - b.1783), 24
BUREN
    Lester (160S - m.1902), 68

BURTBACK
    Margaret (233S), 86
BUSHFIELD
    Gertrude May (322S - b.1876),
        97
BYERS
    Annie M (90S - m.1881), 53

C

CAMPBELL
    Ethel Clark (359S - b.1900),
        103
    Susan M (377S - b.1961), 105
CANARY
    Mary (471S - b.1882), 122
CANFIELD
    Alice M (406S - m.1946), 117
CARMICHAEL
    Annie E (226S - b.1868), 82
CARROLL JR
    John (397S - b.1925), 114
CHAPIN
    Frances Maude (358S -
        m.1892), 102
CHASE
    Lois Gladys (576 - b.1926), 108
    Millard Nelson (394S - b.1905),
        108
    Ruth Jean (578), 108
CHASE JR
    Millard Nelson (577), 108
CHESTER
    Anson J (264S), 88
    Daisy M (482 - b.1875), 88
    Roy (483 - b.1877), 88
CLARK
    Alice (13S - m.1735), 7
    Esther (13S - m.1740), 7
    William (310S), 93
CLARK
    William T (90S - m.1882), 54
CLARK
    Florence Bird (443 - b.1866), 83
CLARK
    Edson L (444 - b.1871), 83
CLARK
    George A (445 - b.1875), 83
CLARK

E

EDDY
  Ethel Randall (361S), 104
EGGLETON
  Phebe Jane (207S - b.1833), 78
EICHENBURGH
  James (- b.1796), 38
  Sarah Catherine (68S - b.1819),
    38
ELLIOTT
  Harriet B (353S - b.1861), 101
EMIGH
  Frederick A (212S - b.1829), 79
EVANS
  Emily Upright (69S - b.1850),
    40
  Israel (- b.1801), 40
EVENS
  Abner Franklyn (171 - b.1857),
    40
  Andrew Jackson (168 - b.1844),
    39
  Elsie Ann (167 - b.1841), 39
  George Nelson (170 - b.1855),
    40
  Isaac (69S - b.1811), 39
  Mary Josephine (169 - b.1848),
    40, 71

F

FAHS
  Alice Reba (358S - m.1922),
    102
FENTON
  Rebecca (- b.1757), 24
FLETCHER
  Unknown (399S), 116
FOSTER
  John (474S - b.1893), 123
  Lydia (645 - b.1921), 123
  Mildred (647 - b.1929), 123
  Vera (646 - b.1923), 123
FOWLER
  Catherine (115S - m.1817), 59
  Charles Butterworth (233S -
    b.1847), 85

Charles Edward (457 - b.1872),
    85
  Cornelia D (454 - b.1867), 85
  David Laverne (459 - b.1876),
    86
  Mary Eva (460 - b.1879), 86
  Minerva May (458 - b.1875), 85
  Rebecca Grove (455 - b.1869),
    85, 121
  William H (456 - b.1870), 85
  Woolsey (310S), 93
FREEMAN JR
  Charles Alden (451S - b.1909),
    121
FREER
  George B (231S), 85
FULLER
  Marion C (311S - m.1873), 94

G

GARDNER
  Aaron (310S - b.1839), 93
  Abigail (33S - b.1764), 18
  Alpharetta (253 - b.1854), 52,
    87
  Andrew J (91 - b.1830), 28
  Anna I (257 - b.1865), 52
  Cecelia (635 - b.1904), 122
  Charles E (254 - b.1857), 52
  Charlotte (643 - b.1914), 123
  Daniel (57S), 29
  Daniel D (- b.1807), 93
  Ella M (636 - b.1906), 122
  Frank (258 - b.1870), 52
  George (639 - b.1914), 122
  George F (470 - b.1877), 87,
    122
  Gerard (644 - b.1917), 123
  James H (256 - b.1863), 52
  Katherine Lydia (637 - b.1908),
    122
  Kenneth (641 - b.1912), 123
  Levi G (255 - b.1861), 52
  Levi Weed (88 - b.1821), 28, 51
  Lydia (474 - b.1894), 87, 123
  Mahala (89 - b.1822), 28, 53
  Margaret (640 - b.1909), 123
  Martha (33S - m.1810), 19

Martha Weed (90 - b.1825), 28,
53
Mary (87 - b.1814), 28
Mary E (249 - b.1846), 52
Richard L (251 - b.1849), 52
Rodger (642 - b.1924), 123
Sadie (472 - b.1884), 87
Sarah M (247 - b.1842), 52
Silas (252 - b.1852), 52, 87
Silas Bond (55S - b.1792), 27
Silas C (33S), 19
Silas Lester (473 - b.1890), 87,
123
Thomas B (471 - b.1881), 87,
122
Wesley G (248 - b.1844), 52
William (638 - b.1911), 122
William G (250 - b.1847), 52
William H (469 - b.1874), 87
GARLOW
Charles G (539), 99
J (331S), 99
Judson C (538), 99
GARRETT
Dorothy (361S), 103
Mary (162S - b.1851), 69
GATES
Frederick (73S - m.1891), 43
GIBBS
Abram L (197S - b.1864), 77
Addie (405 - b.1889), 77
Alice B (409 - b.1905), 78, 117
Anna V (406 - b.1895), 78, 117
Florence (407 - b.1899), 78
John (), 77
Mary (404 - b.1887), 77, 116
Mildred Naomi (408 - b.1904),
78
Nettie Weed (403 - b.1884), 77
GILBERT
Annie (516), 95
Edward (312S), 95
Edward Holmes (518), 95
Grace (517), 95
GLEASON
Robert Hilliard (195S), 75
GOETZ
Charles (361S), 103
GOLDMANN
Christina (415S - b.1897), 118
GOODSELL

Elizabeth Merritt (86S -
b.1824), 51
GOODWIN
Lucile (450S - b.1884), 120
GREENE
Priscilla (397S), 114
GROVER
Charlotte G (366S - m.1899),
104

H

HAGGERTY
Beatrice (500S - b.1901), 126
HAIT
Eliza (116S - d.1891), 59
HALEY
Martha (455S), 122
HAMILTON
Mary Evans (67S - m.1874), 38
HARRINGTON
Mary (301S - m.1869), 92
HARVEY
Clive (392S - b.1896), 107
Norman (574), 107
HAYES
Maria (285S - b.1855), 90
HEFLEBOWER
Annina (502 - b.1875), 92
Emily H (503 - b.1879), 92, 127
Eva (501 - b.1873), 92
John (307S - b.1848), 92
HENNION
Frank (151S - b.1844), 64
Frank Walter (350 - b.1885), 65,
101
Jay O (351 - b.1891), 65
Richard B (349 - b.1883), 64
Robert B (551 - b.1916), 101
HESTON
Delaphine (570 - b.1914), 106
Robert (569 - b.1912), 106
Robert Newton (381S), 106
HEWITT
Unknown (214S), 80
Walter O (420 - b.1858), 80
HIGBEE
Ernest Roswell (395S - b.1913),
108

Keith Herbert (580 - b.1945), 108
Maxine Carol (581 - b.1947), 108
Sylvia Ann (579 - b.1942), 108
HILL
N. Allen (661 - b.1916), 127
Norman A (503S - b.1882), 127
T. Gardner (660 - b.1912), 127
HILLIKER
Frederick (406S - m.1958), 117
HILTON
Ida Elizabeth (332S - b.1865), 99
HOBBS
Caroline (213S), 79
HOLBERT
Allen (603), 117
Darwin (599 - b.1908), 116
Dorothy (600), 116
Earl (601 - b.1916), 117
Florence (605), 117
Ivan (602), 117
Lee (606), 117
Marjorie (604), 117
William (404S - m.1907), 116
HOLMES
Charlotte (311 - b.1822), 59, 93
Gilbert (114S - m.1844), 59
Martha (312 - d.1865), 59, 95
Mary (310 - b.1819), 59, 93
HOOLIHAN
James Michael (382S), 106
HORTON
Phebe (- b.1775), 41
HUBER
William (73S), 43
HULSE
Harvey (- b.1879), 112
Irma L (397S - b.1913), 111
HUNTER
Louise (216S - b.1870), 80

I

IVORY
Increase (158S - m.1861), 67
James (- b.1799), 67
Warren O (363 - b.1863), 67

J

JOHNSON
Charles T (218S - b.1843), 81
Charles T (433 - b.1877), 82
Clara (430 - b.1871), 81
Dr. Charles B (450S - b.1905), 120
Lillie (435 - b.1880), 82
Lizzie M (434 - b.1879), 82
Samuel Hooper (431 - b.1873), 81
Sarah (432 - d.1876), 82
JONES
Patricia Marie (402S - b.1924), 116
JUDKINS JR
Clarence (406S - m.1947), 117

K

KAIN
Fred (169S - m.1911), 72
KANOSPE
Otto (409S - b.1909), 118
KEEFER
Byron F. (268S - b.1855), 89
Eugene G (485 - b.1886), 89
Harold (484 - b.1884), 89
Sidney (486 - b.1891), 89
KELLY
Elizabeth North (), 114
KELSEY
Laura S (330S - b.1853), 98
KEMP
Unknown (73S), 43
KIRKWOOD
Robert (197S - m.1915), 77
KNIFFIN
Martha (41S - b.1760), 23

L

LAFORGE
Isaac (- m.1861), 76
Maria Jane (196S - b.1870), 76
LANE
Charles R (207S - m.1878), 78

MURPHY
Johanna F (320S - b.1889), 96

N

NATHAN
Elmor (385S - m.1948), 107
NICHOLS
Elmira (530), 98
H.F. (329S - m.1874), 98
William R.W. (531), 98
NOYES
Deborah (54S - b.1795), 26

O

OLDHAM
Gilbert Vaughn (499S - b.1878), 125
Gordon V (655 - b.1905), 126
ONUSKO
Eleanor (397S - b.1918), 112
OSBORN
Amos (13S - m.1743), 8

P

PAINE
Mina (311S - m.1889), 95
PALEN
Adelaide (455S - b.1905), 121
PECK
Martha (13S - m.1742), 7
PECK
Hiram V (157S - b.1837), 67
PECK
Prosper (- b.1797), 67
PECK
Emory M (362 - b.1861), 67
PENDLETON
Mary Elizabeth (163S - b.1849), 69
PENNEY
Charles Edward (629 - b.1890), 121
Charles Walter (455S - b.1858), 121

David Benjamin (628 - b.1889), 121
Decatur Butterworth (631 - b.1896), 121
Fanny May (630 - b.1892), 121
John William (233S - b.1861), 85
Jonathan Weed (633 - b.1905), 121
Mary Cornelia (632 - b.1900), 121
Vernon Walter (634 - b.1909), 122
PENNIMAN
Harry (414 - b.1865), 79
Unknown (212S), 79
PETERS
Geraldine (572 - b.1921), 107
Richard D (385S), 106
PHINNEY
Priscilla Joan (397S - b.1925), 114
William Whyte (), 114
PIERCE
Elsie Anna (73S - b.1836), 42
William (), 42
PINE
Elizabeth (157S), 67
POLHAMUS
Unknown (310S), 93
POPP
Joseph (176S - b.1846), 73
William J (388 - b.1884), 73
POST
Charles H (443S), 119
Everts Clark (622), 119
POWELL
Edward (197S - m.1928), 78
PRICE
Marie (269S - b.1875), 89
PRYSTOWSKI
Harry (409S - b.1925), 117

R

RANSOM
Howard Cassius (493S - b.1882), 124
Leroy Howard (652 - b.1907), 125

RAY
    Frank (162S), 69
REICK
    Esther J (382 - b.1896), 71, 106
    Gerald (383 - b.1899), 71
    Sadie M (381 - b.1883), 71, 106
REICK JR
    Frederick (166S - b.1857), 71
REYNOLDS
    Sarah (52S - d.1833), 26
RICE
    Caroline Laura (311S -
        m.1883), 94
    Pearl Amelia (164S - b.1882),
        71
RICHARDSON
    Sarah (- b.1710), 19
    Sarah (15S - b.1710), 11
ROBERSON
    Sarah M (330S - m.1919), 98
ROBERTS
    Adaline (212 - b.1836), 47, 79
    Arthur (426 - b.1903), 81
    Beatrice (614 - b.1916), 118
    Benjamin (213 - b.1838), 47, 79
    Caroline (419), 80
    Charles (217 - b.1849), 47
    Claire Constance (613 -
        b.1920), 118
    Delia (418), 80
    Gertrude (619 - b.1913), 119
    Harry (424 - b.1898), 81
    Henrietta Carolina (612 -
        b.1916), 118
    Henry (215 - b.1843), 47
    James (428 - b.1910), 81
    Jane (429 - b.1910), 81
    John (417), 80
    John (423 - b.1895), 80
    John (78S - b.1808), 47
    John J (216 - b.1846), 47, 80
    Lavinia (422 - b.1893), 80
    Lorraine (617 - b.1929), 118
    Martha (427 - b.1905), 81
    Milton N (421 - b.1889), 80,
        118
    Phebe Ann (218 - b.1850), 48,
        81
    Sarah R (214 - b.1841), 47, 80
    Virginia (616 - b.1927), 118
    Walter (425 - b.1902), 81

    Warren Silas (415 - b.1888), 79,
        118
    William Henry (416 - b.1892),
        80, 118
ROBERTS JR
    William Henry (615 - b.1920),
        118
ROBERTS JR
    William Henry (618), 118
ROBINSON
    Unknown (214S), 80
ROCKWELL
    George W (74S - m.1886), 44
ROOSA
    Ann Eliza (235S - b.1852), 86
RUMPH
    Smiley B (355S - b.1884), 102
RUSGROVE
    Alice Mabel (397S - b.1888),
        111
    Charles (), 111
    Clarence (397S), 112
RUSSELL
    Emma (259S - b.1850), 88
RYAN
    Bridget (446 - b.1871), 83

S

SALT
    Albert L (496 - b.1865), 91, 125
    Daniel Ireland (498 - b.1877),
        91
    Frances M (499 - b.1880), 91,
        125
    Harman Schultz (497 - b.1870),
        91, 125
    Lloyd Bergen (653 - b.1893),
        125
    Lucy Little (654 - b.1898), 125
    Luke R (300S - m.1865), 91
SATTERLEY
    Ellen H (- b.1838), 76
SCHAEFER
    Unknown (399S), 116
SCHICKLER
    Louise Christina (416S), 118
SCHULTZ
    Harman C (299S - m.1866), 91
    William (495 - b.1868), 91

SCHWETSCHER
   Adele (396S - b.1880), 109
SCOTT
   Aintje (- b.1788), 44
   Charles Weed (353 - b.1853),
      65, 101
   Frank (356 - b.1870), 65
   Frank R (552 - b.1889), 101
   George Swalm (355 - b.1856),
      65, 101
   Grace Mildred (554 - b.1894),
      101
   Helen (402S - d.1987), 116
   Henrietta (354 - b.1855), 65
   Howard E (553 - b.1891), 101
   John L (153S - b.1826), 65
   Kenneth A (555 - b.1899), 101
   Minnie (152S - b.1857), 65
   Nellie B (556 - b.1885), 102
   Thaddeus (), 65
SEELEY
   Florence Ann (406S - m.1951),
      117
SELONICK
   Arthur (404S), 116
SHARP
   Mary Ann (156S - b.1842), 66
SHAW
   Frank Creighton (163S -
      b.1874), 70
SHAY
   Adele (341 - b.1863), 63
   Sophia (77S - m.1833), 46
   Unknown (142S), 63
SHERMAN
   Linda (395S - m.1968), 108
SIMPSON
   Joseph A (82S - m.1887), 50
SINSABAUGH
   Charles G (238S - b.1860), 87
   John R (- b.1886), 112
   Lillian B (397S - b.1917), 112
   Nancy (- b.1799), 38
   Nettie (463 - b.1889), 87
SMITH
   Inez N (), 112
   Mary Gertrude (311S - m.1886),
      94
SMITH
   John Floyd (397S - m.1929),
      111

SNIFFEN
   Ruth (397S - b.1918), 113
SPARKES
   Lawrence S (139S - b.1877), 63
STANTON
   Carpenter (138S - b.1830), 62
   Cora M (546 - b.1881), 100
   Jennie K (547 - b.1886), 100
   Peter Cole (334 - b.1857), 62,
      100
   Uriah (33S - d.1810), 18
STEINMAN
   Francis (70S), 41
STEVENS
   Elizabeth (13S - m.1734), 7
STEWART
   Henrietta (216S - b.1839), 80
STRICKLAND
   Ebenezer (33S), 19

T

TERWILLIGER
   Elaine (397S - b.1925), 113
   Priscilla (84S), 50
   Victor M (233S), 86
THOMAS
   Anna Maria (260 - b.1847), 53
   Anthony S (259 - b.1845), 53,
      88
   Elizabeth (67S - b.1809), 37
   Emma J (481 - b.1876), 88
   John W (89S - b.1824), 53
   Myron (74S - m.1875), 44
THOMPKINS
   Jennie M (402S - b.1897), 116
TICE
   Charles Winfield (- b.1811), 97
   Mary Crist (322S - b.1841), 97
   Phebe (71S - b.1814), 41
   Philip (- a.1769), 41
TURNBULL
   Emily (307 - b.1848), 58, 92
   John (308 - b.1850), 58
   Julia (309 - b.1858), 58
   William (101S - b.1824), 57
TUTTON
   John (395S - m.1965), 108

Lewis Horton (397 - b.1887), 75, 110
Lillian Belle (584 - b.1907), 111
Lora Bell (369 - b.1880), 68
Louisa (225 - b.1857), 48
Ludella (440 - b.1893), 82
Lydia (53 - b.1792), 19
Mabel Elsie (399 - b.1898), 75, 115
Margaret L (623 - b.1909), 120
Marie Adele (583 - b.1914), 110
Marie C (524 - b.1893), 96
Marjory Harriet (395 - b.1915), 74, 108
Martha (45 - b.1770), 17
Martha D.F. (544 - b.1887), 100
Martha Jane (99 - b.1824), 29, 56
Mary (125 - b.1822), 34
Mary (21 - b.1719), 7
Mary (3 - b.1639), 3
Mary (51 - b.1788), 18
Mary (61 - b.1776), 23, 33
Mary E (157 - b.1840), 37, 66
Mary E (374 - b.1882), 69
Mary L (329 - b.1851), 62, 98
Mary R (164 - b.1851), 38, 70
Mildred (597 - b.1915), 116
Minnie Gertrude (190 - b.1868), 43
Miriam H (523 - b.1890), 96
Moses (37 - b.1745), 12
Myrtie Delia (191 - b.1868), 43, 73
Myrtle (453 - b.1909), 85
Nancy C (323 - b.1845), 61
Natalie (529 - b.1898), 98
Nathan B (71 - b.1818), 25, 41
Nathaniel (124 - b.1819), 34, 61
Nathaniel (26 - b.1736), 11, 17
Nathaniel (44 - b.1768), 17
Nathaniel King (325 - b.1857), 61, 97
Nellafornia (401 - b.1892), 76
Odell (155 - b.1834), 37
Olive Maud (367 - b.1877), 68
Oliver (199 - b.1863), 45
Ollie R (545 - b.1890), 100
Orlando (302 - b.1850), 57
Orlena (534 - b.1887), 98
Orvilla (364 - b.1866), 68

Raphael Ashton (526 - b.1873), 97
Raymond Hilton (543 - b.1891), 99
Rebecca Noyes (81 - b.1817), 26
Reubin Watson (398 - b.1890), 75, 115
Richard Marshall (582 - b.1908), 109
Robert Lockwood (100 - b.1828), 29, 57
Rosena Jeanette (194 - b.1852), 44
Roy (368 - b.1879), 68
Rueben (28 - b.1740), 12, 17
Rueben (42 - b.1760), 17
Ruth (49 - b.1785), 18
Samuel (- b.1704), 19
Samuel (121 - b.1813), 34, 60
Samuel (14 - b.1677), 5
Samuel (15 - b.1704), 7, 11
Samuel (24 - b.1731), 11
Samuel (33 - b.1758), 12, 18
Samuel (41 - b.1759), 17, 23
Samuel (48 - b.1783), 18, 24
Samuel (6 - b.1645), 3
Samuel B (68 - b.1809), 24, 38
Samuel K (320 - b.1841), 60, 95
Samuel Kniffin (62 - b.1784), 23, 33
Samuel Lockwood (103 - b.1839), 29
Sanford (223 - b.1854), 48
Sarah (- b.1788), 35
Sarah (10 - b.1654), 3
Sarah (123 - b.1817), 34
Sarah (31 - a.1753), 12
Sarah (46), 18
Sarah (50 - b.1788), 18, 25
Sarah Ann (153 - b.1830), 37, 65
Sarah C (180 - b.1843), 41
Sarah E (324 - b.1848), 61, 97
Sarah Jane (318 - b.1838), 60
Silas Gardner (58 - b.1804), 19, 29
Silas Lockwood (102 - b.1835), 29
Susan Ann (104 - b.1841), 29
Susan J (321 - b.1839), 61

www.ingramcontent.com/pod-product-compliance
Lightning Source LLC
Chambersburg PA
CBHW072255270326
41930CB00010B/2381